Kick Ass

Resumes

William E. McClintic

Copyright 2010

Diverger Press

* WARNING *
If you closely follow the directions contained in this book, you will probably get the job you want.

Editor: Stephen S. Horn

Front and Back cover design and artwork: Dorothy Tugwell Pilurs
                                            Jim Pilurs

Large print first edition , 2010, PRINTED IN THE UNITED STATES OF AMERICA

ISBN 13: 978-0-615-36272-4
ISBN 10: 0-615-36272-9

Library of Congress Control Number: 2010925496

Other works by William E. McClintic

Judas The Beloved Disciple Remembered
(Large Print Paperback)

Interviewing For A Job (video & teacher manual)

Motivation...the Basics (video & workbook)

Resume Mistakes (video & handout)

Kick Ass Interviews (in editing)

In memory of Ken Markel and Art Wolfe
friends, colleagues and mentors

For Gregg (Dean too)

Thanks to Charlotte, Liz, Maria and Oliveth

From The Editor:

Hardly a day goes by when I am not asked to help someone write a resume. Ordinarily, the resume books I find are a complicated mixture of psycho-babble and self help jargon. ***Kick Ass Resumes*** is just the opposite. William E. McClintic has distilled the process of writing a resume to its most fundamental, practical, easy to understand level. His tried and true methods are designed to help produce an excellent resume that will give an edge over other job seekers.

Many "business gurus" write books about everything from resumes to auto mechanics. They think of their advice as life changing or even spiritually enlightening. McClintic's many years of valuable "hands on" experience and education have <u>not</u> made him a "legend in his own mind." Instead, he has quietly honed the knack for cutting to the chase and weeding out the impractical and unnecessary fluff that every employer and human resources manager knows all too well.

I recommend ***Kick Ass Resumes*** to everyone who needs a job, not a lifestyle makeover. It is for those who aren't content to sit back on their yacht and wait for the world to bring them a cocktail. This book is for those who need a resume that is accurate, impressive, complete and effective. Indeed, it is for those who want theirs to be the resume that ***Kicks Ass***.

Stephen S. Horn
B. A. Speech Communication, University of Alabama, 1986
M.A. Speech Communication, University of Alabama, 1988
Oxford Fellow, 1999

May, 2010

KICK ASS RESUMES

Table of Contents

Acknowledgements

This effort is the product of more than 30 years of endeavors in the area of "work, job and career" beginning with various typical youth jobs beginning at about age 5 as an "unpaid" helper in my Mother's family truck farming operation where I began learning the value of work and standards by sorting tomatoes into grades and the ownership of work by stamping the business name on each package. It is also a continuation of my advising and assisting others in their world of work.

My background also includes establishment of a career planning and placement office at a college where I was teaching, being a "head hunter" , hiring authority, an employment and training specialist, plus the author of the content of the educational videos *Interviewing For A Job, Motivation...the Basics,* and *Resume Mistakes* along with the manuals and workbooks. I have also been an invited guest speaker on these topics.

I acknowledge the valuable contributions of various employers and supervisors plus peers and members of my staffs. The list would not be complete without acknowledging customers, students and users.

Introduction

Kick Ass Resumes has been written specifically for those individuals who have been in the workforce for a time, but the concepts can be used by anyone seeking a job. In fact, many people who have never worked have successfully developed a resume using the techniques presented in this book in helping them get their first job.

While the majority of the content focuses on a proven manner of preparing a resume that will help get interviews and job offers, other pertinent job seeking information is also presented. The final chapter contains information on the Internet, for example.

There are a few topics in the second chapter that are not exactly about resume preparation, such as the ones on the garbage of being unemployed, the "grieving process" and motivation, but do have a direct or indirect relationship. It is highly recommended that these not be skipped. If you are currently unemployed by layoff, termination, voluntary separation, or simply have never worked before, that chapter should be read thoroughly and the exercises presented should be completed. It is also recommended that the book be used in the following manner:

> 1. The first time through, skim through the book reading the first two or three paragraphs of each chapter to get an understanding of what the book is all about. Skip over the exercises and examples. This initial effort will take only 20 - 30 minutes. Then, put it aside to reflect on what you will be reading.

> 2. When ready, pick up the book and read it through without interruption; it will take about 3 - 4 hours. Read each chapter thoroughly again skipping over the exercises and examples. Make notes of those parts that have special meaning for you. Then put it aside to mentally review what has been read in preparation for doing the exercises.

3. Finally, complete each exercise in the order presented after reading the chapter pertaining to the exercise. Then, actually write your very own *Kick Ass Resume.*

SECTION 1

GETTING STARTED

Chapter 1

What Resumes Are

The title of this book, ***Kick Ass Resumes***, was deliberately chosen to draw attention to, and underscore, the potential power of a well prepared resume in helping you get a job.

A resume is a written document that is a summary or synopsis of you in relationship to the world of work; a brief recapitulation, abridgment, abstract, or précis of your work background. It is a collection of brief statements that provide an introduction of you about your ability to do a job. It is a personal communication from you to the employer.

Your resume should convey much more than simply who you worked for, your title, where you went to school, and what you majored in. **It must clearly state those skills or abilities you possess that will permit you to do the job the employer needs to have done.** The chapter on "skills" explains this in detail.

Employers expect resumes; a lot of employers require them; and many employers want to review your resume before having you come in for an interview for the job. A resume is a given in job hunting.

Because of this, most job seekers have the mistaken notion that a resume will get them a job. There are also scores of authors who have written hundreds of resume preparation articles and books containing advice on how to write a resume that will get you a job. But:

A RESUME WILL NOT GET YOU A JOB !

The best a resume will do, is "sell you" to get an interview to help get a job. Sometimes, even the best prepared resume content will not even do that. Most often, a resume will screen you out, especially if it is poorly prepared. Be sure to read the chapter on resume mistakes.

In today's highly competitive job market, job seekers must sell themselves, and therefore, a resume must be viewed as a piece of sales literature or advertising. It should be written to sell you to get an interview, and sell you after the interview is over.

The average resume receives only 20 seconds of reading time. Within 5 seconds, your resume must not only stand out from the others, it must grab the reader's attention encouraging them to read further.

There are two major reasons why resumes receive such a short reading time. First, most are poorly prepared; some very poorly prepared. While many people think they have a good resume, the majority do not. Often, it is simply how the resume looks, not what it says, that causes the reader to simply ignore it.

80% of an employer's decision to hire is based solely on the appearance and presentation of the job seeker. A resume is an extension of the job seeker. The appearance and presentation of the resume have to be the best possible to just be considered for the interview. To repeat, it is appearance and presentation that are most important, not your experience. Your experience accounts for only 10% of the employer's decision to hire. The remaining 10% is based on things like testing and references. You are, then, responsible for over 90% of the employer's decision to hire.

And guess who controls the appearance and presentation of the resume? **You do!** So it is really up to you to have an effective resume appearance and presentation that causes it to be read. It is up to you to have a resume whose appearance and presentation make it stand out from all the others.

The second reason resumes receive so little reading time is competition. Today's job market is more competitive than ever. For each advertised job, you can be sure there will be lots of people trying to get it.

Recently a major retailer received more than 300,000 resumes and hired only 17 people. A well-known aero-space firm ran one small classified advertisement in one newspaper for one Sunday for one position, and received over 20,000 resumes. Imagine how long it would take an individual to give each resume just a few seconds of reading time. Employers are just too busy with other important tasks.

Kick Ass Resumes will show you how to effectively write a powerful resume that will captivate the reader and sell you. You will learn the common resume writing mistakes; the disadvantages of traditional resumes that can cause you to be "screened out"; how to present your skills and accomplishments that will excite the readers of your resume; and the mechanical aspects of developing your resume. You will also learn how to effectively use the resume in various aspects of your job search efforts.

Preparing a *Kick Ass Resume* takes time. It is something that cannot be accomplished in only an hour or two; or even a day or two. It will take a week or more of eight hour days. **Getting a job is a job**, but the payoff is worth it. Although preparing an effective resume takes time and effort, some worksheets are included to help make your task easier. Once the worksheets have been properly completed, you will simply transfer that information to your resume.

Chapter 2

Begin With The Proper Attitude

This chapter is designed to help you get into the right frame of mind by having a good attitude in order to begin the process of developing an effective, well-written resume.

The Garbage Of Looking For A Job / Being Unemployed

The purpose of this section is to point out some of those negative things that can influence how a resume is sometimes written, and that can surface during an interview. Looking for a job or being unemployed can create negative feelings and attitudes which can unintentionally show up on the resume.

Another purpose is to show you that you are not alone in your feelings. Most everyone else also has them. Finally, the last purpose is to show you a way out.

Looking for a job or being unemployed is one of the worst things anyone must face during their lifetime. It causes us to experience and encounter a lot of garbage; it is not pleasant. It can be degrading, demoralizing, and dehumanizing. Depend on it. At times, it's like being on an emotional roller coaster.

Self-esteem reaches an extremely low level. Our very being is called into doubt. People say things to us that hurt, even those well intentioned individuals close to us. Motivation sinks. Apathy or resignation, a sense of "I give up", sets in. We develop fears.

The biggest fear is that of rejection. We also fear that others are going to be in control or in charge of our job search efforts, that someone will be making decisions not in our best interests. We fear we won't have the right information in the resume, or phrase it the wrong way. We fear that the resume will be misplaced or lost. We fear that someone else may be better qualified. And on and on.

Our sense of self-worth plummets, as does self-confidence. We feel that we are no longer responsible for shaping our own destiny.

We can become easily irritated expressing that irritation in the form of anger. Some cry, if only on the inside. Some people turn to "escape" mechanisms to avoid facing the reality of the situation...sleep, eating, alcohol, drugs, reading and television to name a few forms of withdrawal. Lying can occur, especially to the "self" as well as to others. Some resort to crime as a means of survival. Money becomes a source of great concern leading to confrontation and possible loss of possessions.

Loss of family and friends can take place. A few people ponder and attempt suicide.

What has happened, is that the "garbage" has taken control. And like a big bag of garbage over the shoulder, it weighs us down more and more burdening us with depression and despair.

The Way Out

It is important to share this section and the following worksheet with those close to you so they will know what you are feeling. It is important that you express your feelings and not keep them pent up on the inside. Carefully develop a network of individuals with whom you can share your feelings and who can offer emotional support as it is needed, even late at night. A spouse. A parent. A best friend. A member of the clergy. A confidante.

By completing the worksheets in later chapters on your own personal **skills, assets,** and **accomplishments** your sense of self-worth will increase. They will show that you are a valuable, worthwhile human being that has a lot to offer not only an employer, but society as a whole.

Make a decision to wrest control away from the garbage. An effective way to help do this is to write each piece of garbage on a small piece of paper, then throw each one in the trash. Return the sense of being in charge and in control where it belongs: with you! Another effective method of getting rid of the garbage is to write down exactly how you will get rid of it one piece at a time. Use the following worksheet to develop an action plan for refuse removal, or hazardous waste management.

Garbage Control Worksheet

On the left-hand column of this worksheet, list all the garbage you are carrying, then list how you plan to get rid of it in the right-hand column.

Garbage	Disposal
Have been getting mad	Read anger management articles
Lied to others	Apologize to each one

The Grieving Process

This section is closely related to the previous one on garbage. There is overlap, and each influences the other. Like garbage, grief can exert charge and control with its own negative aspects influencing what is written in the resume.

When people grieve, they are in mourning, sadness, sorrow, and trouble. In short, they hurt. There is a process of different stages that are gone through.. The grieving process is most closely associated with death; the death of someone near and dear.

Elisabeth Kubler-Ross was a pioneer of the grieving process identifying five stages: denial, anger, bargaining, depression, and finally, acceptance. Her work initially concerned the terminally ill and those close to them and her effort has been expanded upon by many others.

The process also occurs at the time of divorce, or when a child leaves the nest, both creating a sense of loss that approaches death.

The loss of job, including voluntary separation, for many individuals, is more traumatic than even death itself. A part of them has "died". Fellow "work family" friends may never be seen or spoken with again; they have "died". Possessions that become lost due to the "lack of job" money crunch have "died". The person who has lost a job may experience a thousand deaths. The sense of grief can be overwhelming, and the process long lasting.

A person who has lost a job will experience one or more of the several different stages of the grieving process, some simultaneously. Those individuals close to the person, such as a spouse, will also go through the grieving process.

The Stages Of Grief

   * **False Elation** During the first few days of job loss, there is a sense of gladness that it has happened. "Gee, I'm glad I won't have to go back to that pit." " I won't have to put up with the crotchety old boss any longer." This false sense of happiness usually disappears when reality sinks in.

   * **Denial** In this stage the person denies, or refuses to recognize or admit, that loss has occurred. "They didn't mean to lay me off; I'll go in tomorrow and things will be the way they were." Normally, this stage does not last long. The quickest way to end it is to realize that the job is gone...there will be no return.

   * **Self-Reproach** Self-blame is another word. Mea Culpa. "It is my fault that I got laid off." Most likely, that is not the case. Today, many organizations are downsizing, rightsizing, streamlining, and belt tightening in order to remain competitive. You don't have to like it, but you don't need to blame yourself.

   * **Blame** Some people attempt to handle their grief by blaming others or a situation for what has happened. "Curse those employees for going behind my back causing me to be fired." "Damn the economy for making me lose my job." Condemning others will not make the fact go away.

   * **Pity** In this stage, the person who has lost a job is seeking compassion and sympathy. A little bit of pity at first is permitted, but don't let it last long. "Feel sorry for me, I lost my job." "Please hire me, I have to support my wife and kids." This stage tends to last longer than the previous ones.

   * **Anger** This one is like a cancer, it consumes the good. Hatred and bitterness show through. "Fire me will you? I hope to Hell the business burns down." It is blame carried to the ultimate degree. The person is angry with everyone and everything, and has usually lost control. It is okay to vent

feelings, to express anger, as long as it doesn't hurt others. The person who gets hurt the most is usually the person who has the anger.

* **Depression** A person who is depressed feels discouragement and dejection. "I don't know what I'm going to do; I don't have a job." "There are no jobs out there." They see no hope. But there is hope. New jobs are being created every day; hundreds of them. There is a good job waiting for you to fill it.

All of these stages need to be worked through before beginning to write a resume or to begin the job search. They must be dealt with. The person in the grieving process needs to get to the final stage as quickly as possible. Until the final stage is reached, the grief and the garbage are in control. That final stage is:

* **Acceptance** In this stage, the person accepts what has happened, no matter how disagreeable, and gets on with the rest of life resuming control of life. What has happened is over; it is history. And like history, we can't go back and change it. It is stamped "approved". We don't have to like it, but we must accept it.

Getting Through Grief

People handle grief in different ways; some of which are as detrimental as the grief itself. There are those individuals, for example, who keep it "all bottled up inside."

As with the section on garbage, if you are grieving, share this section with those close to you. Let them know what you are going through. And, realize they may also be going through the grieving process. Talk about what is happening, how you feel. **Be careful to choose a good time and place to talk!**

Meal time probably isn't a good time. Nor is a few minutes sandwiched into getting ready to take the kids to some event. Choose a quiet time that will be uninterrupted. Select a time and place with no distractions such as a blaring television. A good idea is to talk about when and where you can discuss this important issue.

You may want to choose a "neutral turf" as a place to talk. Try a bench in the park, a walk around a few blocks near home; or the library at church.

It is wise to agree on some guidelines or rules for the talk. How will each of you handle anger should it occur? What about finger pointing and blaming the other person? Remember that each of these is part of the grieving process. Bear in mind that this talk is uncomfortable for both parties.

Select some other people who can provide support. A former co-worker, a teacher, a counselor, a previous supervisor, a friend, or a member of the clergy. And, begin to practice:

Good Grief !

Just as there are opposites in physics, so there are opposites in grief.

* **Joy** It is possible to take joy in job loss, especially if there were aspects that were not likable. It affords the opportunity to do what we really want to do.

* **Affirmation** It is better to declare that the job loss was a good thing to happen. Often, it lets us reach our highest potential possible.

* **Commend** Congratulate yourself that you did the best job you could. That you were not at fault.

* **Respect** Show appreciation toward others for a decision that was difficult for them to make. Most importantly, **Respect yourself** !

* Pride Be proud of the skills, assets, and accomplishments that you have, some of which were probably gained on the job you lost.

* Calm Instead of exhibiting anger, try composure and tranquility; be at peace. Reach through to your spirituality.

* Optimism Look on the bright side of things. Be positive, not negative

By practicing "good grief" the process will be easier to get through, and that final stage of acceptance can be reached more quickly. Part of a popular song several years ago sums it up rather well: "You got to accentuate the positive; eliminate the negative; and don't mess with Mr. In-between."

Having the proper attitude is essential in developing very good resume, a *Kick Ass Resume*. Getting rid of garbage and leaving the grieving process behind are major steps in having a good attitude.

MOTIVATION

A major component of going forward with life and job search is understanding motivation. While motivation is a major topic in a variety of areas, one of critical importance is that of job...employment...working. Employers are seeking motivated people to work for them. Most organizations want people that are self motivated.

Motivation is not just one isolated thing, or caused by one isolated thing. It is several things together. Motivation is what moves us as individuals to action. It is what causes us to do something; a driving force. It is a prompt, inducement, purpose, impeller, reason, cause, impulse, or stimulus. Motivation comes from within, but is reinforced and influenced from without.

A knowledge of motivation can assist us in understanding our own behavior and actions; it is part of self understanding. That knowledge can help us to also understand the behavior and actions of others. The knowledge can help improve how we interact and get along with others. These are things the employer wants to know.

The basics of motivation can best be comprehended by first understanding "needs". A person's "needs" are the primary motivator. "Needs" are different from "wants", which are also motivators, but not as strong as "needs", the most powerful motivator.

Several years ago, Abraham Maslow set forth a theory of motivation based on "needs". *Maslow's Hierarchy of Needs* was part of the theory and graphically depicted as a pyramid divided into five segments from top to bottom.

Many people, over time, have made adaptations to Maslow's Hierarchy. The following information is based on *McClintic's Hierarchy of Needs* which builds and expands on Maslow's.

MASLOW'S
HIERARCHY OF NEEDS

```
        /\
       /S A\
      /------\
     / ESTEEM \
    /----------\
   /    LOVE    \
  /--------------\
 / HEALTH & SAFETY \
/------------------\
/ BASIC PHYSIOLOGICAL \
```

Basic Physiological Needs: The first level , the foundation of the pyramid, is called "Basic Physiological Needs" and they are powerful motivators. These needs are what a person needs to survive such as food, clothing and shelter. Having food is a "need"; having steak is a "want". Having food is necessary for survival, steak is not. Clothing is a "need"; having 10 pairs of shoes is a "want". Shelter is a "need"; owning a home is a "want".

Basic physiological needs vary around the world and in each country; sometimes by season of the year. The clothing needed in Wisconsin is different from that needed in Egypt. The clothing needed during the winter in Wisconsin is not the same as that needed during the summer. Needs change.

It is important to note that both "wants" and "needs" are goals or objectives to be achieved. A specific goal or objective can be one of the most driving motivators. **However**, that goal can become a fixation or obsession

Health & Safety Needs: Once most, if not all, of the basic physiological needs have been satisfied, a person is then motivated to fill the "Health & Safety Needs". We all have a need to be healthy and safe; strong motivators.

We have a need to live in a place free from predators and people harming contaminants. We need protection from disease and pests. While we need food to survive, we have a need for the food to be healthy. We have a need to be free from danger. We need to be secure and safe from harm. We need protection from bodily injury.

When we are endangered or hurt, we need access to whatever is necessary to prevent the peril or heal the wound.

"Health & Safety Needs" motivate us to acquire those things that are essential for survival beyond our "basic physiological needs". They vary from region to region, and change based on our age or state of life.

Love Needs: Once most, if not all, "Health & Safety" needs have been met, a person is motivated to satisfy the "Love" needs. We all have a need for affection; and it is a potent motivator. We have a need to be liked, to be shown kindness, to be needed.

Before we can receive love, we must be capable of giving love. Before we can give love, we have to be able to receive it. Before we can either give, or receive, love we have to love our self. We have to accept the "self" for who and what we are at any given point in life. That is not to say that the "self" cannot, or should not be improved.

If we need to be liked by someone, we need to be able to accept it, and need to be willing to return it. But first, we need to like our "self". This also means that we need to accept the other person for who and what they are.

Consciously, or unconsciously, we are all motivated by our love needs. Camaraderie, trust, loyalty, a sense of belonging, friendship, sociability, intimacy and kindness are some examples of "Love" needs.

Esteem Needs: After most, if not all, of our love needs are satisfied, each of us has a need to be held in esteem, an influential motivator. We have a need to be respected, to be valued, to be held in regard. We have a need to be admired, honored, appreciated and treasured.

There is a fine line between "Love" and "Esteem" needs. In fact, it is probably a dotted line, if there is any line at all; they are so closely related.

Like love, before we can receive esteem, we have to be capable of giving it. Before we can give it, we must be able to receive it. Before we can give or receive esteem, we have to respect the "self". This respect is called "self esteem".

On the job we have a need for esteem. We liked to be thanked by our boss and peers for a job well done. We need to be appreciated for our efforts. When those things happen, we are motivated to do more, and do it even better. We all like to receive "warm fuzzies", those things that make us feel good.

Self-actualization Needs: At the top of the pyramid is "SA", "Self-actualization" a term coined by Maslow. It is a very powerful motivator. Being self actualized means being happy. It means being successful; by your definition, not someone else's.

Self-actualization means being proactive rather than reactive. You make things happen rather than waiting for something to happen then reacting to it. It means developing the total self to the highest level possible.

A self-actualized person is confident, sure, positive and assertive; not negative or aggressive.

Each of us has needs for being self-actualized, and all of us are self-actualized to some degree; some more than others.

A person does not really progress from level to level. We always have the five needs presented thus far and are motivated to fill them. At different points in our lives, based on what is going on in our lives, we place a greater or lesser amount of emphasis on a specific needs area.

If a self-actualized person experiences one or more negative encounters in the esteem area, reprimands by a supervisor for example, that individual will place a greater emphasis on the esteem needs. It does not mean that the person is no longer self-actualized. It merely means that the person is placing more importance, has more motivation, to rebuild esteem.

A person who has just been injured, or someone close to them has been, is motivated to readjust the health and safety needs. It does not mean that the individual is no longer self-actualized , or no longer has esteem.

When a person loses a job, that person may be motivated to reorganize several needs levels. Esteem will need attention. The individual will be concerned about basic survival placing emphasis there and on health and safety needs plus love needs. It does not mean the person is no longer self-actualized.

McCLINTIC'S
HIERARCHY OF NEEDS

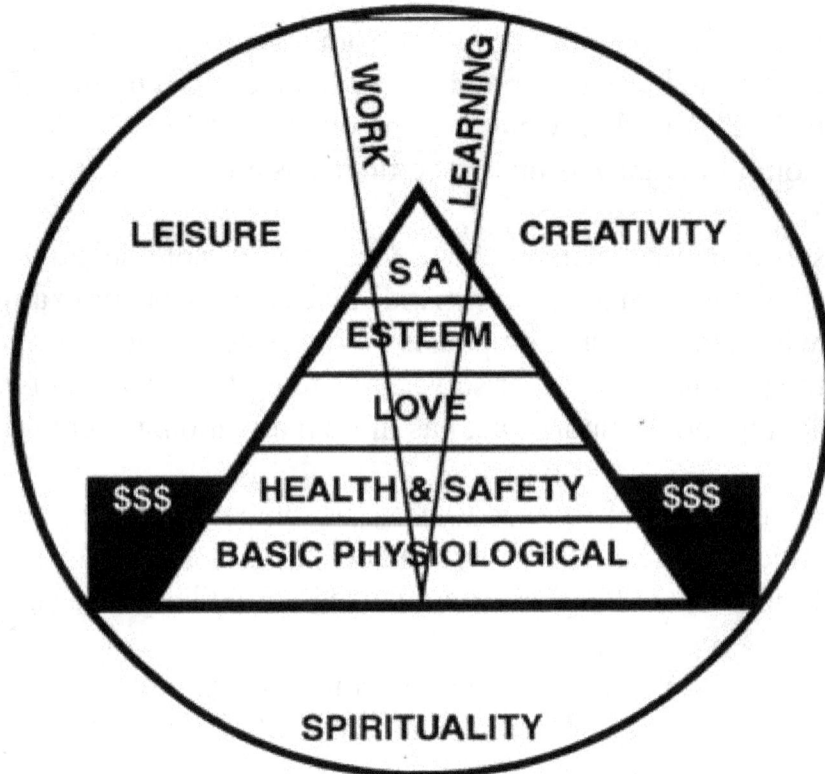

Learning Needs: The first part of McClintic's Hierarchy is a reverse pyramid. The right side of this represents "Learning Needs" which are puissant motivators. (At this point you may have the learning need to know what "puissant" means. While you are motivated, there will be a pause so you may consult your dictionary).

Learning includes formalized education and training. Learning is a life-long process and we have a need to acquire knowledge. Simply put, we have a need to know and are motivated to learn. What and how much varies from person to person. We even have a need to learn how to learn.

Each of us learns in a variety of ways and have a need to learn in one or more specific ways. We learn in school. We learn informally from other

24

people such as friends, even in school. We learn by ourselves. We learn from training including "on-the-job" training. We also learn from books, movies, television and the internet.

The things or subjects we need to learn also vary from person to person. And, as we learn new things, we discover that we have a need to learn other things and are motivated to do so. It is through learning that we acquire skills.

There is a relationship between learning needs and the needs previously presented. Note that a significant part of self-actualization involves learning. When we learn, we are also involved with esteem needs, especially self esteem.

Work Needs: The left side of the reverse pyramid represents our "Work Needs". Each of us have needs to make or do something, and these are mighty motivators. We have a need to be productive. We have a need to use our energy to accomplish something.

We have a need to perform, to fashion, to act, to serve. In part, it is by our work that we are known. We have a need to expend effort, either physical, or mental, or both.

Work is achieved on or off the job. The skills that we have acquired through the fulfilling of our learning needs permit us to work. We are motivated to work in order to utilize the skills we have acquired. We are also motivated to work to help meet our esteem needs. Work also helps us meet our love or affection needs. Our health and safety needs are met in part by work, and so are our basic physiological needs.

Notice that as we progress up the original pyramid of needs that a greater amount of each is met by both our work needs and our learning needs. At the bottom of the first level, basic physiological needs, little is met by our work and learning needs. But at the top level, self-actualization, almost all of it is involved with learning and work.

Money Needs: We have a need for money, it cannot be denied; and it is a motivator. Money needs, however, need to be kept in proper perspective. First, we need to realize what money is: a medium of exchange or trade. It is true that money doesn't buy everything.

Since we need money, we are motivated to trade our "work" for it. Since someone needs work accomplished, they are motivated to exchange their money for your work. The amount of money you receive is dependent on the type, quality and quantity of work you give. Sometimes we trade our work for indirect money. An example of this would be employer paid insurance.

When we have obtained the money we need, we then trade or exchange it for things we need that we are motivated to fill.

Notice where the "money" dimension falls within the hierarchy. This is to illustrate what motivational needs money will help satisfy. We can use money to meet our basic physiological needs such as food, clothing and shelter. Money will help fulfill some, not all, of our health and safety needs. We can purchase medicine or locks for doors.

We can use money to help meet only a small part of our learning needs. We can pay for tuition, books and paper. While we are receiving money from our work, we can, in turn, use money to help meet part of our work needs. We can buy hammers, nails and computers plus much more.

Leisure Needs: Man has a need for leisure, and this is noted on the left side of the pyramids. It is an effective motivator.

Leisure is a time to be at rest, to relax, to take a break, to recharge ourselves, to not be hurried, to play, to be amused, the opportunity to stop and smell the roses along the way. To paraphrase: all work and no leisure makes a person a dull individual. The reverse is also true: all leisure and no work makes a person an incomplete individual.

And, yes, some people are able to turn one aspect of their leisure into work getting paid for it. And some get paid well, very well.

Creativity Needs: The next dimension of the hierarchy, on the right side of the pyramids, is "Creativity Needs". It is one of the most powerful of all motivators. People have a need to be creative, and it is what sets them apart from the rest of the animals. We have a need to think; to reason.

We have a need to use the mind, and it is a terrible thing to waste. We have a need to be imaginative, to conceive ideas, to solve problems, to be inventive, to deduce, to devise, to discover.

As we satisfy our creativity needs, we use them in our work and in our learning. There is a synergy that occurs. Our needs and motivations together are greater than the sum total.

Spirituality Needs: We all have "Spirituality Needs", the most powerful of all motivators surrounding all else.

It is in the spirituality dimension that we formulate our ethics, morals, principles and values. It is here that we develop our conduct of life; where we separate "right" from "wrong". Our virtue is formed here, as is our sense of what is just, what is fair, what is honorable. Our personal integrity is created here.

Spirituality helps us bring order out of chaos. It helps us to answer the unanswerable. In the time of crisis, we reach through to our spirituality. It is in this dimension that we develop our self-control. It is here that we have an ever increasing deposit of a sense of humor.

Our spirituality is dynamic, not static, changing as we receive new information. And, spirituality differs from person to person; no one's is identically the same as another individual's.

Our needs do not exist solely by themselves. They are influenced by, and dependent on, other individuals. For example, parents are motivated to help children satisfy their basic physiological needs by providing food, clothing and shelter. Employers are motivated to help employees have a healthy and safe environment in which to work.

When someone new comes into my social circle, I am motivated to help that person meet their love needs by welcoming them into the group.

If my team scores a touchdown, I am motivated to help their esteem needs by cheering; which in turn can motivate them to score another. A teacher can reward a student's effort building esteem ; which in turn can motivate even more effort. A supervisor's positive comments to an employee for a job well done can help fill that person's esteem needs motivating to accomplish even more.

Motivation is an integral part of each of us that is based on our needs and wants. It makes us who we are.

Chapter 3

Resume Mistakes

The majority of resumes do not even get completely read by employers because they contain one or more of the 22 common errors when prepared. Before preparing your resume, it is important to know about the different kinds of common mistakes many people make in writing their resume so that you may avoid making the same ones.

1.   **Too long** Many resumes are too long to even be considered by an employer. If your resume is more than one page, it is too long. Employers are busy and do not have the time to read lengthy resumes. The average resume receives only 20 seconds of reading time.

Henry Ford once told a salesman that if he couldn't write his sales pitch on the back of his business card, then he needed to rewrite his sales pitch. Your resume is your sales pitch; it is your "business card". You must write it to not exceed one page.

Some employers handle resumes in this fashion: 1 pagers are put in the first pile; 2 pagers are placed in the second; those that are 3 or more pages are placed in the filing cabinet. If enough resumes from the 1 pagers are selected for further consideration, the 2 pagers also are then placed in the filing cabinet without even being looked at.

2.   **Not oriented for results** Your resume must be oriented for results. It has to "sell" you to get the interview, and continue to sell you. The resume should be so written that the employer will read it being sold on your abilities enough to have you come in for the interview; and when the interview is over, the employer will continue to be sold by your resume to the point of offering you a job.

The primary result you want from your resume is to get an interview.

3.   **Red flags** Most resumes, especially the traditional chronological resumes, contain "red flags". A red flag is any information that could screen you out. Red flags are those things that would create questions in the mind of the employer that you could not do the job effectively; that you could not get along with others; that you could be a threat to their job; that you have some deep, dark secret in your background; and so forth. A time gap in employment history is a red flag. Being over qualified or under qualified are also red flags. Even the organizations you have worked for, where you went to school, and what you studied could be red flags. Here are some examples:

If there is even a one month gap in employment history on your resume it can raise a red flag. If the position requires a Bachelor's degree, any more or any less education can be an "over qualified" or "under qualified" red flag.

A person with good sales management experience was applying for a position as Vice President of Sales with other organizations. Near the top of her resume she listed her education stating that her major area of study was music! Most business presidents looking for a Vice President of Sales screened her out because they were looking for someone with a major in business, sales management, marketing, or the like.

In the hiring process, a phenomenon called "transference" takes place. The hiring authority transfers his or her feelings, including prejudice and bias, to you. If you state on your resume that you worked for the ABC Company, and the employer was fired by ABC, what do you think your chances are? The same holds true if ABC is six months late in delivering a critical component, or is behind in paying their account.

If you are applying for a position as an accountant with the accounting manager, and your resume indicates that you have been a Vice President of Finance, you have raised two red flags. One, the accounting manager will see you as a threat, and two, the employer thinks that as quick as you find a better position you'll be gone.

4.   **Not edited or proofread** Before submitting a resume to an employer, it must be proofread several times...by you and by others. There should be **NO**...repeat...**NO MISTAKES**. One person's resume had a job objective of "file clerk" spelling it FIL, and further stating that she had a lot of experience in FLING. In the employer's mind if the person can't spell, the person can't file.

Another sent a resume to be an executive secretary. While her resume stated that she was good at spelling and grammar, grammar was misspelled. Both of these resumes had red flags that screened them out because they weren't proofread.

5.   **Misdirected** Many resumes are misdirected by the way they are written and who they are given to. If you are seeking a job in auto repair and your resume is filled with jobs and experience in only "flippin' burgers" you have a misdirected resume. It should contain only information directly related to your abilities in auto repair.

If you are seeking a job in computer data entry and you send your resume to the personnel manager, it is misdirected. It should be sent to the data processing manager.

Members of the personnel or human resources staff <u>do</u> <u>not</u> have the authority to hire anyone in almost all cases. Their primary function is to screen you out!

6.   **Poorly prepared** If you take the time to write a resume, it should be properly prepared. A poorly prepared resume will screen you out. It is a red flag. I once received a resume that I knew was a resume only because it said so at the top. It was a hodgepodge of information that did not make much sense. It was a very poor presentation with an even worse appearance. Remember, 80% of the employer's decision is based on appearance and presentation.

7.   **Generic** A lot of people screen themselves out by writing a "handy dandy, multi-purpose, one does it all" kind of resume. They then take it to a printer to have hundreds of copies printed, using that same resume to apply for all types of different jobs.

A resume should be prepared for each and every job being sought!
Not to worry, you will be shown how easy this can be.

Don't use a resume that stresses your accounting background if you are seeking a job as a salesperson. Even if you are seeking a job in accounting, a separate resume must be written for each position. One organization may be more interested in your accounts receivable background, while another in your general accounting experience, one in credit, one in tax, and yet another in accounts payable. The requirements for each position will vary from organization to organization.

8.   **Overwritten** For some reason, many individuals think that they must use big words and flowery language in writing their resume. They will use $5 and $10 words when a good 25 cent word will do just as well, if not better. Employers can see through this attempt to impress and screen you out. Try to write the way you talk and usually write.

9.   **Tries too hard** Don't oversell yourself when writing your resume. The old saying is true...you can't make a silk purse out of a sow's ear. If you are a cook, don't write your resume as though you were an executive chef or a food and beverage manager. If you are a copy-writer, don't convey that you are an advertising director.

As much as possible, the real you must come through in your resume.

10.   **Disorganized** Your resume should present information in a logical, organized format; it needs to have focus. The employer doesn't have time to search for the facts. Far too many resumes appear as if the job seeker used a shotgun to scatter the information on the paper. What is needed is a rifle shot approach, each item right on target in or near the bull's eye.

11.   **Too sparse** There just isn't enough specific information for an employer to make a decision to bring you in for an interview…it doesn't sell. Some people have resumes that are three pages long that don't contain any information that the person can do the job. Others have resumes that could have been written on the back of the stamp used to send it.

12.   **Irrelevancies** If an item in your resume has nothing to do with the job being sought, it doesn't belong. Height, weight, marital status, hobbies, and the like are irrelevancies. An employer has a job that needs to be done, and your resume must show that you can do it. Irrelevancies take up valuable space on your resume; space that you need for your unique sales features. Having the heading, **RESUME**, at the top is irrelevant.

13.   **Messy** Ink smudges, type-overs, stains, food particles, lines that go beyond the margin, inserted hand-written words, and so forth make a resume look messy. Employers will view you as a messy person and screen you out. They will think that you don't care much about your resume, don't care much about yourself, and care even less about the job.

An employer once told me after being hired that another person might have been more qualified than I was since that person had a Ph.D.. The employer said that the other person's resume immediately went into the file cabinet because in the middle of the resume was a big circle of coffee stain.

14.   **Unexciting** A resume needs to create excitement for the reader. Many resumes seem to be no more than a collection of mundane words; they are drab and dreary. The words do not entice the reader to give the resume more than a cursory glance.

The use of "action" words will help add excitement to your resume. The mechanical appearance can also add excitement. When you add excitement, the employer is being sold.

15.   **Wrong kind** Your resume must be the right kind. The traditional

chronological resume used to be what employers wanted. Not any longer. When given a choice, 95% preferred *Kick Ass Resumes*. There are still a few hiring authorities such as some government agencies, accountants and engineers that prefer the chronological. For those that do, that is what you should provide.

16.   **Unclear job objective** Too many people have an unclear or too generalized job objective near the top of their resume. After reading the objective, the employer can't determine what job, or even what kind of job the applicant is seeking. They often look like this:

"Seeking a challenging position with a growing company that will let me use my talents and abilities to the highest level possible resulting in mutual rewards with the opportunity for advancement in the continual achievement of personal and organizational goals."

Sounds good, but what the does it really say? I've seen it on thousands of resumes submitted for all kinds of jobs. Just to see what the response would be, I've often been tempted to send out some of my resumes that would say:

"Would like to get a boring job with a company going down the tubes where I wouldn't have to work and still be paid mega-bucks."

17.   **Written by someone else** You must write the resume yourself. Employers can usually spot a resume that has not been written by the job seeker, and immediately put them in a file cabinet. You can get suggestions and advice, but the words must be your own.

18.   **Negative tone** Nothing will screen out a job applicant more quickly than a negative tone. Some people list reasons for leaving each job they have held. Often those reasons convey a negative attitude toward an employing organization, the products or services, the supervisor, or fellow employees. Employers just don't hire negative people. Even though nothing disparaging is specifically stated, the choice of words can convey

negativity. Anything negative reflects on you.

Passed over for promotion...efforts undermined...philosophical differences...coulda... woulda...shoulda. Having three jobs in 2 years or five in 10 conveys the negative "job hopper" label.

19.   **Doesn't sell** There may be a lot of words on the paper, but the resume just doesn't reach out and grab the reader. It doesn't command attention. It doesn't spark an interest. It doesn't create a desire to read it, let alone bring the person in for an interview. There's no electricity. It's b-o-r- i -n-g.

20.   **Contains political or religious information** Nearly all employers are uncomfortable with any mention of political or religious persuasion in a resume and will not consider a person for the job because of it. They can be red flags. It is fine to have political and religious beliefs, but they do not belong in a resume unless you are applying for a position with a political or religious organization.

21.   **Mentions money** The mention of what you have earned, or would like to earn, should be omitted from a resume. It can screen an individual out of even an interview, because the person does not fit into the wage range for the position.

22.   **Ineffective communication** Most resumes do not communicate effectively, yet a resume is a means of personal communication from you to the employer. Therefore, that communication must be effective. A recent survey of employers found that:

The number 1 reason why people aren't hired is poor communication skills!

And, communication is one of the major attributes an employer seeks in a prospective employee. Proving that you have effective communication skills begins with the resume. Each word and phrase must be carefully chosen to communicate exactly what you want the employer to know about you.

Be careful not to indicate that you have good communication skills as an attribute, only to poorly communicate with your resume.

SECTION 2

SELF ASSESSMENT

Chapter 4

EXPERIENCE

The information on self assessment contained in Section 2 is the most important part of developing *Kick Ass Resumes*; everything else is built upon it.

A good sales person knows the product being sold inside out. You are selling yourself to get a job, and must know exactly what it is you are selling. Each chapter in this section is part of determining what you are selling and how to sell it. There is a very important side benefit to you...you will be developing the best awareness of yourself as an important individual improving your self esteem, increasing your confidence, and having greater motivation.

The employer, as buyer, is interested in the **PS** of what you are selling; that is **P**ersonality and **S**kills with an emphasis on both. This chapter begins the process by identifying your skills (experience) background (you began the personality identification in the chapter on attitude). To assist you in this, a worksheet is provided in the Appendix.

You should go back in your personal history as far as you can remember when listing your experiences on the worksheet. Whether they are job related at this point or not, or whether you enjoyed them or not, write them down. Include things from school, church, scouts, jobs, social events, athletics, hobbies, and other activities. Try not to omit anything, even what you didn't like or enjoy. You might want to have headings for each on your "experience worksheet" to assist in organizing your thoughts. Your worksheet may start out something like this:

SCHOOL:

Learned punctuality and attendance importance
Getting along with others
Math through trigonometry
Ran for class treasurer
Following instructions
Following a routine
Answering questions
Write book reports
Science
Tennis team

Making friends
English
History
Tried out for cheerleader
Reading a blueprint
Asking questions
Debate team
Homework
Share & Tell
Prom committee

CHURCH (Synagogue, Mosque, etc.):

A sense of right and wrong
Values
Morals
Code of conduct
Respect for fellow "man"
Sold at bake sale

Developing a life style
Ethics
Spirituality
Reading topical material
Sang in choir
Acted in play

SCOUTS:

Doing things with others
Earned merit badges
Making things
Getting along with others
Following directions

Helping others
Camping
Live by a code
Manners & etiquette

JOB (include all, even if you weren't paid):

Baby-sit
Doing what was asked
Communicating with others

Deliver papers
Keeping records
Getting along with others

Sold magazines (maybe as part of school)
Punctuality & attendance
Operating cash register
Being honest
Make change
Take messages
Keep my work area neat
Dress appropriately
Work safely
Keep inventory
Buy things
Use calculator
Sort mail by importance

Persuading others
Following instructions
Answering phone
Making reports
Use a computer
Being polite to customers
Use a hammer
Punch a time clock
Plan ahead
Restock items
Be organized
Package products
Meet deadlines

ATHLETICS:

Teamwork
Follow directions
Show others what to do
Keeping Healthy
Sportsmanship
Accepting loss

Learn rules
Coach little league
Avoiding injury
Fitness
Being a gracious winner

Social Activities might include: building a snow fort; hosting a party; writing "thank you" notes; being a club member; getting along with others; and participation in events.

Chapter 5

Skills

The skills you possess are a very important part of your resume. Skills are what employers want to find out about you. Skills are what you should "sell" and emphasize in your resume. Skills were learned and used in every aspect of your experiences that you just listed!

An employer has a job that needs to be done, and it is your skills that permit you to do the job. The greatest fear an employer has is that you can't do the job. Your resume must sell you based on your skills. Each skill you present in your resume is a sales feature. How you present those skills can minimize or eliminate the employer fear that you can't do the job.

A skill is an ability. A skill is something learned through your experiences. It is a talent you possess. There are thousands of skills, and the average individual possesses a few hundred. Though no longer published and declared obsolete by them, the US Department of Labor in their *Dictionary of Occupational Titles* set forth that there are three categories of skills: people, data, and things. They also developed general competency levels for each category with examples of each. The information is still available on line through the efforts of private enterprises; and can be accessed by entering the book title in the various search engine lookups.

Among others, **people** skills include providing information, advising. consulting, bargaining, and supervising. Some of the **data** skills are sorting, posting, gathering, analyzing, and correcting. **Things** skills cover abilities such as assembling, operating, inspecting, and driving.

There is a worksheet in the Appendix to help you prepare a list of at least 100 skills that you possess including a description or definition of them. On completion, you will have a list of 100 sales features that can be used for your resume, in a cover letter, during the interview, and in the thank you follow up letter. Each skill should be phrased in as positive a manner as possible. In describing each of your skills, you should try to paint a word picture for the reader.

Typing is a skill, but merely stating **typing** on your resume doesn't sell. If you qualify and quantify your description, it will. **Typing of data and documents** does a better job. **Typing of data and documents with speed and accuracy** is better yet. **Typing of data and documents with speed and accuracy in an office environment** is even better. **Typing of data and documents with speed and accuracy in an office environment to 70 words per minute with zero errors** gives an employer a clear understanding of what the person's typing skill is all about. With the word picture created, the employer can visualize the writer of the resume sitting in the office doing the job. The employer is being sold; is having the "can't do the job" fear eliminated, and starting to make a favorable decision to hire before ever meeting the individual.

Filing is a skill, but doesn't say much. **Filing of information by alpha, numeric, and geographic in a rapid manner using a format for easy retrieval** says it better.

In the space below, create a word picture for the skill of **report writing.**

Report writing

When preparing your resume, do not list your skills in the order you have written them on the worksheet. Instead, when you write your resume, present them in the same order of importance as they are sought by the employer. The skill that is number 26 on your worksheet may be the number 1 skill the employer is seeking, or the number 3 skill on your worksheet is not on the employer's list at all.

Employers usually list the skills being sought in the order of importance in the job description or advertisement with the first skill listed being the most important. And, the order of importance will be different for each employer.

It is important to remember that some skills are job specific, while others are transferable. "Posting" would be a job specific skill for a bookkeeper. "Micrometer usage" would be a job specific skill for a tool and die maker. Mathematic skills are used for both jobs and on almost every kind of job; so are writing skills.

The American Society for Training and Development, ASTD, which is comprised largely of employers, in conjunction with other organizations, has developed a list of transferable skills employers want. If these are skills employers want, be sure to list them on your worksheet and resume.

Part of the secret of *Kick Ass Resumes* **is to give employers what they want!**

Skills Employers Want

Learning to Learn Employers want to know if you have the ability to learn. Have you learned how to learn? Do you know how to ask questions. Do you know where to find answers? How fast do you learn? What is the best way for you to learn? Each of us learn in different ways. Some by trial and error. Some by reading. Some by seeing. Some by being told. Some by a combination of ways. On your worksheet it <u>might</u> look like this:

Learn quickly keeping abreast of new developments by reading 3 trade journals and belong to the area job association.

Write one that pertains to you

3 R's: Reading, 'riting, and 'rithmetic These are the basics. At what level do you read, write, and perform math functions? Can you read <u>and</u> understand what you have read? Can you write so others do not mis-understand what you have written? Employers are not looking for an Einstein or a Hemingway. Most will be happy if you can perform the basics at the 7th grade level. Also, consider that probably 90% of all jobs can be performed by anyone with a 7th grade education. On your worksheet it <u>might</u> look like this:

Write copy for catalogs in a descriptive and easy to read manner.

Prepare one of your own.

Communication This includes your listening and speaking abilities. Can you understand what someone else says? Can you respect someone else's opinion even though it may not agree with yours? Can you tell someone else your thoughts so they understand what you are saying? On your worksheet it <u>might</u> look like this:

Utilize effective 2-way communication in all interactions with others.

How would you phrase one of yours?

Problem Solving Your problem solving skills permit you to use your ability to find answers to questions or a dilemma. Can you find solutions? Do you possess the knack to find answers quickly? Can you identify the problem? Can you distinguish between a problem and its symptoms? On your worksheet your description <u>might</u> look like this:

Proven problem solver possessing the ability to isolate the cause identifying alternative solutions suggesting the one best to resolve the issue to the benefit of all concerned.

Try writing one for you:

Creative Thinking Creativity is what sets man apart from other animals. It is the ability to use the imagination. Can you visualize things in your mind? Can you relate concepts to each other? Can you use your mind to take A and B to get C, or even bypass C to get D or E? Your worksheet description <u>might</u> look like this:

Proposed 3 new products using product segmentation and product differentiation.

Let your creativity show:

Self Esteem Self esteem is having respect for yourself. It means to accept yourself for who and what you are, being proud of all the good parts while striving to improve the weaknesses. Are you confident? Do you have self-control? Do you like yourself. It <u>might</u> look like this on your worksheet:

Possess good self-image being confident doing what needs to be done to the best level possible.

How would you describe your self-esteem?

Goal Setting Goals are motivators, and employers look for motivated employees. Goals are objectives or ends to be met. An employer is interested in your ability to establish realistic goals for assigned tasks, and your ability to achieve them. One <u>might</u> look like this on your worksheet:

Can establish realistic goals enjoying the challenge of task completion.

Explain your goal setting attributes:

Personal and Career Development This means having a continuously revised plan of growth for yourself and your job/career. What have you accomplished in these areas in the past? What do you have planned for the future? Your worksheet entry <u>might</u> look like this:

Enrolled in an *Adobe 9.0* class to be at the latest state of the art.

Phrase one of yours here:

Group Effectiveness This aspect conveys to an employer how you function or behave in a group. Do you blend in? Are you a team member? Do you tend to withdraw? Can you make a new group member feel at ease? How do you react when the rest of the group wants to go one way, while you want to go another? Your worksheet entry <u>might</u> look like this:

Team player striving to achieve group consensus.

Write your attributes here:

Interpersonal Skills This attribute considers your interaction with others on a one-on-one basis.
Can you get along well with others? Do you offer praise and encouragement? Can you offer and accept constructive criticism? How do you handle situations where someone makes you angry? A worksheet entry <u>might</u> look like this:

Get along well with others being receptive to constructive criticism.

How would you phase your interpersonal skills?

Negotiation The ability to interact with others to reach an agreement is negotiation and usually involves give and take for those involved. Are you willing to compromise? Can you make trade-offs? Can you bargain? Are you willing to concede one point to gain three? A worksheet entry <u>might</u> look like this:

Spearheaded committee to develop new order processing format that all agreed on.

Set forth a description of your negotiation abilities:

Organizational Effectiveness An organization is a collective entity comprised of individuals wherein the whole is usually greater than the individual members. Are you at times willing to put the good of the organization above your own self interests? Do you come to work early? Stay late on occasion? Can you offer suggestions in a positive way that will improve the organization? Here's an example:

Proposed new phone system to improve external communications relieving pressure on the switchboard.

What might you explain?

Leadership This is the ability to guide, conduct, or influence others. It means getting work done through the efforts of others. Leadership does not mean that you're the boss. Employers are not looking for each employee to be the next Bill Gates or Stephen Jobs. Can you set an example? Can you provide direction to others? Can you show someone how to do parts or all of their job? An example of how it <u>might</u> appear on your worksheet:

Chosen to train new sales staff on all aspects of each product.

Write one for you:

These are some of the many transferable skills employers seek in addition to job specific skills.

Whenever possible, use "action" words in your resume. Employers are looking for people of action. Action words help make your sales features exciting. Action words help sell the employer. The Appendix contains several action words to help you describe your skills.

Chapter 6

Assets

The assets you possess are also a most important part of your resume. In the final analysis, assets are really the most important items the employer uses in determining to hire you. Often, an employer will hire a person with better assets and lesser skills than a person with better skills and lesser assets.

An employer's second biggest fear is that you cannot get along with others and be easily supervised; that you won't fit in. How you present your assets can minimize or eliminate this employer fear.

Assets are your human interaction skills and personal attributes. Assets tell an employer about the "personal" you; your "person"ality. Assets indicate whether or not you can get along with fellow employees...if you are a team player...if you can easily be supervised. They also include what are referred to as your self-management skills. These would include punctuality and attendance. It is through the presentation of assets that you convey your work ethic to the employer. Frequently, an employer will hire someone who has a better work ethic over a person who has better job skills.

Some of the skills you have already listed on your skills worksheet are properly labeled "assets", and belong in this section. Simply lift them from the "skills" worksheet and place them on the worksheet for assets which is part of the appendix. Another step in identifying your assets is to list on the worksheet everything that others have said in describing you including teachers, friends, supervisors, and others:

"Good listener. Smiles a lot. Optimistic. Firm but fair. Not one to gossip. Good moral and ethical convictions. Gives and earns respect. Sensitive to others. Willing to go out of the way to help someone. Patient in teaching tasks to others. Well mannered saying please and thank you. Homework is always on time or before due. Does not interrupt.

Conscientious in all efforts."

Like skills, assets should also be qualified and quantified wherever possible not simply making one word statements. Some examples:

Require minimal supervision	Maintain strict confidentiality
Never lose temper even when provoked	Adhere to personal code of ethics

Possess good sense of humor

It is interesting to note that 85% of employers say that they look for a sense of humor in a prospective employee. If that's what they want, you need to let them know you have it. Curiously, few resumes contain any reference to humor.

Each asset you describe on your worksheet is a sales feature, and again, you must sell yourself. The asset list you develop will be used not only for preparing your resume, but writing the cover letter, during the interview, and the thank you follow-up letter as well.

The Appendix contains an Asset listing of areas of human interaction skills and personal attribute areas that can help the employer make a hiring decision in your favor.

In the space below and on the worksheet in the Appendix, describe each of your assets. There are many, and each person has quite a few. Try to identify at least 50. Each one you list on your resume may be just the sales feature that the employer is seeking that would give you an advantage over other people seeking the same position. When describing your assets, use as many action words as possible being sure to paint a word picture for the employer trying to qualify and quantify each one when possible. Be sure to create a computer document for reference keeping it up-to-date.

Asset

Asset

Asset

Asset

Asset

Asset

Asset

Asset

Asset

Chapter 7

Accomplishments

Accomplishments are your achievements. They are results of your actions. You use your skills and assets to make an accomplishment. Accomplishments tell an employer how well you are able to use your skills and assets.

By presenting your accomplishments on your resume, you are selling the employer how he or she and the organization might benefit from hiring you. Presenting benefits to a buyer is a proven sales technique. The employer is the buyer; you are the seller. You are selling your skills, assets, and accomplishments to the employer.

Like skills and assets, accomplishments should be qualified and quantified creating a word picture for the employer.

When presenting your accomplishments, try to choose words that will imply or infer a supervisor's reward, feeling, or decision. Some words that do this are: chosen, selected, appointed, and awarded. Using these types of words convey that someone else thought so much of your skills and assets that they chose to reward you.

Supervised a staff of 8 sounds much better when stated as: *selected to supervise a staff of 8*. By using the word "selected", you are stating that someone else thought so much of your talents that they appointed you to this position. You are using a subtle testimonial. You are letting someone else help blow your horn. You are letting someone else help sell you. Though that person is not identified by name or position, that person is helping the employer reach a decision to buy your talents.

Accomplishments are achieved not only on the job, but in other activities as well. Accomplishments are something you are proud of and can be achieved in school, sports, volunteer work, and the like. While all accomplishments are important to you, some may not be meaningful to an employer. You want to list on your resume only those non-job related achievements that have a relationship to the position you are seeking.

Listing your accomplishments may sound like bragging. It is!

For some unknown reason, most of us have been instructed to be humble and meek in our job search efforts. But don't be. It is not only permissible, but preferable, to boast about those things we have achieved. Just exercise care.

Accomplishments are worthy of pride, after all, and you are merely showing that pride to an employer in a manner that will help the employer to decide you are the best person for the job. Besides, if you don't brag about you, who will?

Each of us have many accomplishments in our background. As you list yours on the accomplishments worksheet, it may be helpful to refer to the list of jobs you have ever had to reflect on what accomplishments you had for each one. You can do the same for school, volunteer work, and similar activities you have been involved with.

Perhaps you received a certificate for attendance at school. This can be phrased as: *Awarded certificate for perfect attendance*. Here are some other examples:

Elected chairman of health and safety committee. (Could have been at church).

Reduced accounts receivable 53% improving cash flow 21%.

Cited for proposal reducing scrap 15% resulting in $37,000 annual savings.

Promoted to head product design group of 12 staff members.

Appointed to spearhead comprehensive EPA report of 496 pages.

Your accomplishments should be hard-hitting, yet concise, again painting a word picture for the employer. Try to limit them to one line as much as possible. You should be able to compile a list of 25 accomplishment sales features for your resume. Describe your accomplishments on the worksheet in the Appendix and transfer that information to a computer file for ease of retrieval keeping it up-to-date.

Chapter 8

Deciding What You Want To Do

To this point, you have developed a pretty good grasp of what you have been and what you are. It is now time to determine what you want to do. You now have the opportunity to take charge and control of the rest of your life. Part of this is to get a job you will be happy with. A good portion of success in life and on the job is simply being happy.

Far too many people are really not happy with their job, or kind of job, and should be in some other type of endeavor to use the talents possessed. Typical excuses for staying in the same kind of work: "That's all I know. That's what I studied to be. I'm too old to try something else. The pay isn't as good. My friends would laugh at me."

Even if you truly want to stay in your type of occupation, there are many options available to you. A nurse, for example, can consider employment in a hospital, doctor's office, nursing home, school nurse, military, county health department, industrial nurse, home health care/visiting nurse, teaching nursing, and selling nursing supplies to name a few choices.

Before preparing your resume, you must decide what kind of job you want, then target your resume to that kind of job. There are 12,741 different types of jobs according to the old *Dictionary Of Occupational Titles* (DOT). One is just right for you. The hard part is deciding which one, but it is not that difficult. There are several methods of determining which one.

1.   Discuss your skills, assets, and accomplishments with others. Review your worksheets with them. Ask them what types of jobs these fit.

2.   Write what you would consider the ideal job description. It should contain many of your skills and assets while capitalizing on your accomplishments. There is a worksheet in the appendix for this purpose.

3.   Review your experiences, skills, assets, and accomplishments worksheets by yourself. Place them side by side on the table, floor, or bed letting your eyes wander over them. A gestalt, or pattern, should emerge. There is a thread of commonality that runs through them. It may strike you like a bolt out of the blue...."why didn't I ever think of that type of job before."

4.   There are several career interest inventory assessment devices that can point in the right direction. The counseling or placement office of a school or college is a good place to check them out. Don't forget the library. Some of the internet sites involved with job/career offer these also.

5.   Some companies have produced computer software programs that can help you in determining job options. Some will let you enter a variety of options or parameters such as skills, growth, and salary then search the software database for the jobs that meet your criteria.

6.   Career counselors are another resource to assist in job type determination. Check the local Yellow Pages. Some charge a fee. Don't overlook your local job service office, or the career counselors at educational institutions. Some states have established "one stop" career centers that not only have counselors to provide you with advice, but also have a library of books, magazines, videos , the aforementioned career assessment devices, and computers with lots of career related software. These centers are often listed on the internet.

7.   Many books have been written to aid in job type determination such as the old *DOT*, *Occupational Outlook Handbook* (updated every 2 years), *Guide For Occupational Exploration*, and *What Color Is Your Parachute* (revised annually, and often on the best seller list). There are books about jobs in specific career fields such as medical, technical, and manufacturing. There are even books about jobs that require less than a college degree.

8.   Perhaps the right job for you is to be in business for yourself. If this is

true, you will still need a resume. Bank officials and others will want to know all about your skills, assets, and accomplishments to help them make decisions in working with you. The library will have several books on running your own business that will list the skills you will need to have. There are even books on franchise opportunities.

Should being in business for yourself be your goal and you have no experience in the type of business you want to have, it is strongly suggested that you spend some time working for an organization to obtain a reasonable background in operating that type of business.

9.   Informational interviews are yet another method of determining the right job. Make appointments with employers for a few minutes of their time to discuss job type options for you based on your skills, assets, and accomplishments worksheets. This sometimes results in a job offer! And by all means leave a copy of your resume.

10.   If you are in the proper age group, you may want to consider the military. Discuss your options with a recruiter, and read some of the books in the library about careers in the military. The military does offer some very good benefits.

11.   Not to be overlooked are temporary staffing and employee leasing firms. Many of these organizations have positions to fill up to and including senior level management. Some even offer a good benefit program and provide training.

12.   Surf the Web. The Internet contains a tremendous wealth of information plus a wide variety of career and job determination assistance. Read the chapter on it at the end of the book.

When determining the ideal job for you, consider "trade-offs". We make trade-offs throughout all aspects of our life, and choosing the right job is no different. You might want to consider a job utilizing some skill to a lesser degree, but one that affords a greater emphasis on an asset.

Another factor to consider in deciding what you want to do might well be the return to school, or the securing of training. A myriad of options exist to assist you in this endeavor at little or no cost! Such a choice would permit the acquisition of new skills that will make you a more valuable choice for the company you want to work for.

NOTE THIS: It is almost imperative that you have the skill of operating the ubiquitous, pervasive **computer** ! Computers are used almost everywhere in the world of work. It is essential that your ability to use a computer is up-to-date and kept up-to-date.

Our Changing Economy

The changes that have been taking place in our economy should be considered in determining the kind of job you want to get. We are now in a global economy that is highly competitive and undergoing dynamic change. At times it is highly volatile with dramatic impact on the workforce. All of this can have an influence on your job determination, resume, and job search efforts. Some characteristics are listed below.

There will be fewer big and middle size businesses as mergers continue and some organizations simply cease to exist.

More small organizations will appear and will continue to employ the majority of workers.

Businesses are relocating or opening branches around the world.

There is extreme competition for jobs even as hundreds are created each day.

There is no job security.

People will be changing careers, not jobs, every 3 years.

New skills are coming into being, and some existing ones are becoming more widespread, such as the variety of computer skills.

More jobs will require bi-lingual or multi-lingual abilities.

Individuals will be changing jobs every year.

Today's hot companies and hot jobs may be tomorrow's cold ones.

There are geographical "hot spots" for employment.

Yesterday's area of slump is today's place of boom.

People will work later in life.

There will be more minorities in the workforce.

There will be more job seekers with a disability.

Transferable skills will be needed.

More jobs will be temporary and part-time.

More employers will permit work-from-home.

There will be more self-employment.

Organizational lay-offs will be more frequent.

Relocation may be required.

75% of new jobless are white-collar and gray-collar.

There will be more youth seeking jobs.

There will be an emphasis on "Sell American".

Less than 50% of working adults will be in a full-time job with one employer.

There will be fewer employee benefits.

There will be more foreign competition for jobs.

New types of jobs will come into existence. There are so-called "futurist" organizations that prognosticate what types of new jobs there will be and what skills will be needed.

Education , training, and learning will be life-long just to keep abreast of changes.

A high percentage of new businesses fail the first year.

More foreign ownership of American businesses.

Greater influx of foreign nationals seeking jobs.

More job opportunities in other countries.

Employers will place greater emphasis on the personal attributes and human interaction skills (assets) of employees.

One major aspect of our changing economy is elimination of positions within industries. Listed below are specific industries with significant job loss projected for the next few years; this does not mean that there will be no job openings. There will be, but the job may be short-lived.

| Wired telecommunications like land line phone | Printing and related firms including book publishers |

Department stores	Cut and sew apparel manufacturing
Motor vehicle	Semiconductor
Newspapers	State and local governments
Postal services	Mining

There are specific jobs that have a gloomy outlook that need to be considered in deciding what you want to do. Some of the following jobs may almost be extinct in a few years.

File clerks	Telephone/switchboard operators
Data entry clerks	Bank tellers
Travel agents	Mail clerks
Video store clerks	Photo Processors

GOOD NEWS There are a few job sectors that are hiring employees now and need additional staff members.

Health care	Federal Government (Not post office)
Social Assistance	Life Insurance Agent
Vocational Rehabilitation	Employment Services
Educational Services	Computer Systems Design Services

SPECIFIC COMPANIES HIRING RIGHT NOW
According to Forbes on April 2, 2010

Best Buy
Tyson Foods
Lowes
Comcast
Apollo (Univ. of Phoenix)

Express Scripts
Siemens
United Health
Amazon
Costco

Chapter 9

Determining What Employers Want

Determining what employers want is ignored by 90% of job seekers! Yet, it is one of the most critical areas in all your job search efforts and of immense value in preparing your resume. If you don't know what they want, it's much harder to sell them.

Watch any good sales person in action. One of the first things done is to determine what the buyer wants. You began your efforts in this area by completing the exercises on the items set forth by the ASTD in the chapter on skills.

To further determine what an employer wants will require some research and digging for information to develop the background necessary to prepare your resume. The information you seek can be remembered by the acronym J O B. It stands for the three categories of information you need to have. In addition to the resume, you will use that information to help write the cover letter, prepare a thank you letter, and to interview for the position.

J is for job

O is for the organization and its products and services

B is for the boss and co-workers

The job is not just any job, but the specific one you want with a specific company. You will need to know what the position is all about. While the no longer printed *Dictionary Of Occupational Titles* and the *Occupational Outlook Handbook* (both developed by the U.S. Department of Labor) can provide very good general information, it's only a start.

Most organizations have written job descriptions. Try to get one for the job you will be applying for. Usually all you have to do is ask for it. As an aside, job descriptions usually list a salary or wage range, Most of the time the job description will have the duties and requirements written in rank order with the most important listed first, the next most important will be second, and so on.

When you prepare your resume for that job, you will want to put your skills, assets, and accomplishments in that same rank order. If the ABC Company is seeking a computer data entry person with the first qualifying requirement being keyboarding skills of 10,000 strokes per hour, and that's the job you want, you don't want to lead off your listing of skills with "operate a variety of computers" followed by "proficient in WORD"!

Another way to gather the information you are seeking is to simply ask questions. "What would be my three most important tasks?" What are you looking for in someone for this position?" "Would you describe other people who have held this job?"

Jobs do not occur in a vacuum, but with organizations, and you want to know as much about the company and its products and services as possible. The Internet and the library are good places to start gathering this kind of information. There are books that detail information about specific organizations. Your librarian will be happy to direct you to the publications you need. The library may even have a copy of the firm's annual report or a shareholder prospectus.

Annual reports contain valuable information. Sometimes they reveal particular problems, new products to be introduced, and the like. You may have a background that addresses these issues that you would want to include in your resume. The organization may also have a company newsletter that probably contains information you can put to good use.

Asking questions can provide you with a lot of information, and don't be afraid to ask them. Ask questions not only of organization members, but customers, suppliers, and competitors. Where do you think the organization will be five years from now? Who are your three major competitors? How would your customers describe your products and services? Is there any major problem you are experiencing? Can you tell me about your organizational philosophy?

Finally, the "B" stands for boss and co-workers. Try to obtain as much information about them as possible. Again, asking questions is a good way to gather it. Talk to people you know who work for the organization. If you don't know anyone who works there, ask friends and relatives if they know anyone who works there. The reference books at the library, annual reports, and company newsletters often contain at least a few of the names of an organization's employees.

If you are unable to identify anyone who works for the firm, try asking the receptionist. The receptionist often knows more than anyone else in the organization, and may provide you with not only the name of the supervisor for that type of position, but also the names of other employees. The receptionist may even answer some of the questions you have.

How would you describe the boss' supervisory style? How would you describe the other employees in the department? What happened to the person who held this position previously? How does the supervisor react when something goes exceedingly well? Goes wrong? What does the boss do in a typical day? What are the major strengths of the best employee in the department? What skills do you use most?

Send each person a thank you letter.

Getting the answers to these questions can help you in writing your skills, assets, and accomplishments for the resume you will prepare for the specific job. You can then fine tune them so they are phrased to your best possible advantage. The information can also be used in drafting your cover letter, writing a thank you letter, and during the interview. When writing these documents, try to provide answers to questions you would be asked in an interview. The employer will always have questions, and you can refer to your documents to obtain the answers needed to reach the best decision for the good of the department and the organization as a whole.

A recent survey of hiring authorities, supervisors and managers, disclosed what the top ten things they wanted in people they would be hiring:

1.   **Good work ethic** doing more than just enough to get by, concern for quality, good work habits such as timeliness, and pride in a job well done, beginning to work at starting time, not leaving early, reliable, dependable, follows rules and policy, doesn't spend much time in non-job related "chit-chat", doesn't waste time and effort.

2.   **Positive attitude** cooperation, willing to take supervision and suggestions, fairness to self and other employees plus the company, not grumbling or whining, no back-stabbing, not finding fault with others, cheerful, optimistic, avoids negativity.

3.   **Self motivation - self starting** suggest what to do next instead of waiting to be told, enthusiasm, willing to try, proactive rather than reactive, accept responsibility.

4.   **Willingness and ability to learn** can learn new procedures and methods, willing to try the new company's way, attempt new things, open to training.

5.   **Loyalty** interested in organization success, faithful to peers and supervisor, maintain confidentiality, dedicated.

6.   **Team work** cooperation with others, not selfish, more concern with team goals than self objectives, constructively contributes at meetings.

7.   **Experience** having the needed skills to do the job without a lot of supervision or training, (note that it doesn't say employment background).

8.   **Education and training** formal or informal learning of the necessary

knowledge and acquisition of abilities.

9.   **Honesty** does not "b---s---", does not blame others, does not cheat or steal, does not ask someone to "cover for me", does not lie, has personal ethics, has integrity.

10.   **Ability to solve problems** can generate alternatives and solutions, knows difference between symptom and problem, recommends improvements.

You should be aware that employers not only want you to have these attributes, what they don't want is the opposite. These need to be conveyed in your resume. Complete the worksheet in the Appendix on what employers want.

SECTION 3

FOCUS ON *Kick Ass Resumes*

Chapter 10

Types Of Resumes

There are only a handful of different types of resumes: ***Kick Ass Resume***, Functional (also called a Skills Resume), Chronological, Combination, Gimmick, and Curriculum Vitae. Most employers prefer the ***Kick Ass Resume***, but a few do prefer the others.

The ***Kick Ass Resume*** is the best type for a job seeker since it eliminates most, if not all, resume mistakes when properly prepared. It is the easiest to develop as a piece of advertising or sales literature. Because most employers prefer them, and because they are the best at selling you this is the type to develop.

The ***Kick Ass Resume*** is basically a functional or skills resume that zeros in on a specific job. Not a type of job, but a specific job with a specific organization. This type resume is prepared for each job applied for since each job has different requirements with different organizations. If you apply for five jobs, you need to prepare five ***Kick Ass Resumes***. If you apply for ten, then you need to prepare ten. Yes, it will take some time and effort, but both will be reduced because you will simply lift the information already compiled on your worksheets.

This type of resume stresses your skills which is really what an employer wants to know about you. It emphasizes that you possess the abilities to do the job that the employer needs to have done. It also highlights your accomplishments which indicate to the employer how well you can do the job.

By listing your assets, this type of resume lets the employer know how well you will fit into the organization and how well you will get along with others. It therefore minimizes or eliminates the employer's two biggest fears: that you can't do the job; and that you can't get along with others.

Employers really don't care who you worked for, when you worked for them, who your supervisor was, where you went to school, how much education you have, and when you got it.. Again their primary concerns are can you do the job and get along with others.

In short, the *Kick Ass Resume* will provide the employer with the necessary information about you so that you will be brought in for an interview.

The Functional or Skills resume is just that...a listing of the skills you possess. The skills may or may not be qualified and quantified. It is usually preferred to the Chronological by job seekers because they can cover up things like time gaps in employment. It is also easy to prepare an original and have multiple copies made. The disadvantages are that the Functional resume does not let you tout your accomplishments, or let you stress your personal attributes. Should you decide to develop this type, try to include some of your accomplishments and some of your personal attributes in a sense turning it into a modified *Kick Ass Resume*.

The Chronological resume used to be the preferred type and is still erroneously used by many job seekers because they think that is still what employers want. In the final analysis, a Chronological resume is based on time to a large degree. Dates are very important. When did you go to school? How long did you work for your last employer, and each one before that. It basically follows the same format as an application. And, **an application is designed to screen you out!** A Chronological resume will also screen you out. Too many red flags are raised, each one being a reason for an employer to not bring you in for an interview let alone consider you for the job.

By its format, you really can't sell yourself with a Chronological resume. The typical format is an Education heading followed by where you went to school; what you studied; and the dates attended. Some add grade point average and class standing.

Next comes Employment, or Work Experience as a heading. Then the dates of employment for each company you worked for; the name of the organization; your position or title; and a brief description of your duties. Employment is presented in reverse chronological order beginning with your current or most recent employer.

It is difficult to sell yourself with a Chronological resume. It is nearly impossible to develop one as a piece of advertising. It's traditional format practically precludes citing your skills, assets, and accomplishments. Should you prefer to prepare one, however, try to include as many of those sales features as possible turning it into a modified *Kick Ass Resume*.

The Combination (Functional/Chronological) resume tries to make the best of both worlds. Education is listed first followed by a listing of skills and ending with employment history. While perhaps more advantageous to you than a traditional Chronological resume, it contains the disadvantages of both. Again, should you select this format try to include some of your most important assets and accomplishments.

Curriculum Vitae is Latin for "course of life". This type of resume is just like a Chronological only more detailed and longer, usually running to a few pages. It is rarely used, and then for only specialized kinds of jobs such as University Professor. It has several of the disadvantages of the Chronological, however it does give you the opportunity to mention your skills, assets, and accomplishments.

A Gimmick resume is just that, a gimmick. A resume is prepared that has one or more clever schemes in the hope that it will stand out from the rest of the resumes an employer receives and will be remembered. Once in a while they succeed, but mostly they fail.

This type may involve the use of paper that is slightly larger than the standard 8 1/2 x 11, or paper that is an unusual shape or paper of a very loud color such as chartreuse. One enterprising person submitted a resume in a tennis shoe with a card attached that noted, "Just trying to get my foot in the door." Unfortunately for the sender, it was an old, well used sneaker that smelled like it was over-used creating a rather odious odor in the employer's office. Result? No interview.

One lady submitted a resume for a position as an airline flight attendant that was on the back of a photograph of her...a full frontal nude pose. No interview.

Another, applying for a job as a wine salesperson, had her resume carefully prepared and affixed to a wine bottle in place of the label sending it to the sales manager. She not only got the interview, she got the job because no one else was considered any further.

About *"Job Objective"* ... Replace It With *"Summary"*

Most authors of resume books and staff members of organizations that assist in resume preparation indicate that a heading of **Job Objective** or just **Objective** at the top of the resume is needed. There are a variety of reasons for not doing this which were alluded to in the chapter on resume mistakes.

First, many job objectives are poorly written; even by those whose job is to professionally help you to prepare a resume. Most of the job objectives read like this:

"Seeking a challenging position with a growing company where my talents and abilities can be utilized for mutual benefit and reward leading to increased responsibilities and advancement."

At first glance it sounds good. But it isn't. It really doesn't say anything. There is nothing about the job seeker. It doesn't sell the job seeker. It's too generic. That objective could be used by anyone applying for any kind of job with any kind of company. As an employer, I seldom read that type of objective, and frequently did not read the resume. I suspect other employers do the same.

A better job objective would state exactly the specific position desired: accountant, engineer, waitress, file clerk, copywriter, or lifeguard. It could be improved by citing some specific talents and abilities: month-end close processing, designing conveyor systems, providing cheerful service, filing by alpha-numeric, proficient at editing, or Red Cross certified.

Another problem of using a job objective is that you are telling the employer what you want to be instead of what you can do.

Having a specific position in your job objective is limiting and can keep you from being considered for other positions. In effect, you may have just screened yourself out. For example, if you state that your objective is a sales position, you probably would not be considered for sales management or sales promotion even though you may be well qualified to perform such a job, and may even prefer such a job. It could even pay more!

Should you state you are seeking a position in accounts receivable, you have probably eliminated yourself for consideration in accounts payable, general accounting, or accounting management.

Summary is recommended as a heading in place of Job Objective. A summary is an abstract, brief, recap, synopsis, or an abridgment of your background. It is a resume of your resume.

Your summary should be one to three hard-hitting, incomplete sentences that capture the basic "work" you. It should tell what you can do and have done. What you are, not what you want to be. If you reduce your resume to those one to three hard-hitting sentences, you would then have a very good summary. Some examples:

SUMMARY: Strong "from scratch" food preparation background from appetizers through desserts utilizing strict adherence to recipes possessing experience in all forms of cookery with an emphasis on Cajun and Creole.

SUMMARY: Professional secretarial experience with the ability to calmly handle an extremely bustling office and specializing in the prompt preparation of error free detailed legal documents.

SUMMARY: Skillful automotive engine repair with a background in the latest state-of-the-art diagnostic devices with yearly update training by major manufacturers particularly in the area of diesel.

SUMMARY: Experienced fine-grade paper technology chemist awarded 3 patents possessing hands-on laboratory background and proven success in supervision of process control.

SUMMARY: Computer programming experience from PC to main-frame using "C", FORTRAN, HTML, and COBOL for financial institutions, especially credit unions, with an emphasis on remote network interconnect using XENIX, LAN, or Ethernet.

SUMMARY: Effective apartment maintenance experience including electrical, plumbing, carpentry, and grounds for multi-unit complexes to 700 units willing to be on 24 hour call.

While Summary appears near the top of your resume, you should probably write it after preparing the other sections which will make it easier. As you write the Summary, as with all sections, carefully choose the words used. It is the "sizzle" that sells. Use descriptive adjectives and adverbs. While what you say is important, it comes down to how you say it that can make the difference.

Practice writing your summary several times. Change the order of the phrases. Change words. Can you say the same thing, but say it better?

SUMMARY:

SUMMARY:

SUMMARY:

SUMMARY:

Chapter 11

Putting It Together

To this point you have completed the necessary worksheets to prepare a **Kick Ass Resume** that will sell you to get an interview: Summary, Accomplishments, Skills, and Assets.

But before you begin putting it on paper, put yourself in the shoes of the employer receiving your resume. The "Summary" and the "grabber" need to contain the hooks that capture attention encouraging further reading of your resume content. Be careful to avoid jargon that might confuse the reader. Be honest in the facts you set forth.

Now try to get it down on paper, for practice, and on one page after reading this chapter by utilizing the worksheet in the appendix.

Do not put the heading, **RESUME**, at the top. The reader will know what it is. Besides, it only takes up room...room that you can better use to sell yourself.

The first thing that needs to be on your resume, at the top, is called contact information. That includes your name, address, and phone number. The employer needs to know how to reach you. The employer can't contact you to come in for an interview without it. Your contact information can be centered, to the left, or to the right. To leave more room to sell, try to get it on one line or two, three at the most. It might look like one of the following:

John Doe * 123 Easy Street * Omaha, NE 12345 * 312-555-1212

Jane F. Smith

907 South Main	**888-555-7340 (work)**
Plains, MI 07318	**888-555-4321 (home)**

Alvin K. Folderol
5455 Front Road * Sofa, IA 32154

909-555-9090 (home)
909-555-0909 (work)

ROBERT (BOB) JONES
555-535-4918

2640 Brill Rd. Muncie, ID 744996
bobj@cyber.net

Next comes the **SUMMARY:** heading followed by the one to three hard hitting sentences that capture the basic work you. Simply pull this from the worksheet you have already completed.

ACCOMPLISHMENTS: is the heading for the next entry followed by 10 to 15 transferred from your worksheet. If you prefer, you may use the heading, **ACHIEVEMENTS:** in place of accomplishments.

SKILLS: are listed after accomplishments. Use 10 - 15 from your skills worksheet. You may also call them **ABILITIES:** if desired.

The last heading is **ASSETS:** which can be completed by inserting 10 to 15 from your assets worksheet. Your rough draft resume now contains 30 - 45 sales features.

At this point your rough draft practice resume should look something like the following:

YOUR NAME * ADDRESS * PHONE NUMBER(S)

SUMMARY: The one to three hard hitting incomplete sentences that capture the basic work you.

ACCOMPLISHMENTS:
   * A listing of 10 - 15, more if you so choose
   * That are based on your skills and assets **painting a word picture**
   * So the <u>employer understands</u> how well you work
   * Each one is a **sales feature**
   * Selling you to get an interview

SKILLS:
   = These are what employers want to know
   = They want to know if you have the **abilities to do the job**
   = The employer's biggest fear is that you don't
   = So **sell them** that you do!

ASSETS:
   + Are your personal attributes and
   + Your human interaction skills
   + That <u>minimize or eliminate</u> the employers fear
   + That you can't get along with others

Notice that it is somewhat unbalanced. It lacks something. That something is called a "grabber". It is a one line statement about you, or a work philosophy you hold. It might look something like these:

Treat each and every individual as a worthwhile human being

Dedicated to doing the job right...the first time

Without excellent customer service, no one has a job for long

This addition helps balance the page making it more pleasing to the employer's eye. The grabber must be written very thoughtfully with attention to you and the job being sought. Often, it is the summary and the grabber that the employer remembers. People tend to read the first and last items, sometimes skipping the middle. Whatever is at the bottom of your resume must be a sales feature helping to draw the reader back to the total content of your resume.

The headings presented such as **SKILLS:** help organize and focus your resume content. It has a logical format. It is easy to follow the information presented. The reader can quickly refer back to a section of the resume at a later date to find information for clarification or confirmation purposes.

No, the recommended *Kick Ass Resume* format does not include education. The content already indicates that you are a person of intelligence. Your education can be mentioned in the cover letter, or addressed in the application. Nor does it include references or the statement, "References Furnished On Request." The employer already knows that if you are asked for references you will provide them.

It also does not provide a listing of personal information. Many employers receiving resumes containing personal information such as age, marital status, and the like immediately reject them to avoid inadvertently facing possible charges of discrimination in the hiring process.

While hobbies, interests, and leisure activities may be important to the employer, questions on these topics can be asked during the interview, and need not be included in the resume unless directly related to the job.

Some Tips

When actually putting your resume together, use the following tips to help your resume stand out even more; to help it sell better; to help make it more memorable.

Incomplete sentences, though not grammatically correct, should be used.

Action words and the use of adjectives and adverbs can make a dull resume exciting. They add "sizzle". There is a list in the appendix.

You will want some words and short phrases to stand out. Consider all capital letters, underlining, and bold or Italic type face.

In selecting the overall typeface, choose one that is easy to read, and pleasing to the eye. Some recommended ones are: Times New Roman, Arial, and Verdana. Have a printer or computer whiz show you samples pointing out the advantages and disadvantages of each. The font size should not be less than 10 and 12 is recommended.

The use of "bullets" is quite effective. For your accomplishments try using an asterisk or star (*). Sometimes there is an unconscious sales activity involved. Each time the employer sees a star, that will register, or underscore you as a star. For skills, you may prefer the equal sign (=), indicating that you are equal to the task. For assets, you may want to try using the plus sign (+). Each one will register in the employer's mind as a plus, reasons to interview and hire you. Avoid using bullets that may have a negative connotation such as the minus or the zero.

Try drawing a rectangle around information groups such as **SUMMARY:** It is eye catching, and helps further convey that you are organized. Employers don't hire people who are disorganized.

While resumes with black ink on a good white paper are always acceptable, give consideration to using a soft pastel paper with a contrasting ink...soft gray paper with cobalt blue ink; a cream or buff paper with brown ink; pale green paper with a dark green ink.

Employers are conservative, and some more than others. Certain professions also tend to be more conservative such as accountants and engineers. Be sure your resume is tasteful, not gaudy.

Use margins or border space. The left and right should be the same, as should the top and bottom. This also provides the "white space" that helps make the resume easier to read.

When developing your accomplishments, skills, and assets phrase statements, try to write them so they don't exceed one line; two at the most for just a few.

Have nothing in your resume that would cause the reader to question your credibility. Avoid any information that can indicate religious beliefs, political persuasion, ethnic origin, and the like, especially activism pertaining to some cause.

Edit your resume with extreme care. Watch spelling. Avoid shifting tenses between past, present, and future; keep it the same throughout. Look at each word to determine if another word could be used to better effect. Then edit again. Then have someone else edit it. Utilize "spell check" on the computer.

Use a computer as much as possible, if you don't own one try the school or library. You can always rent. Some print shops have computers that you can use for free or at minimal cost. You can put your worksheet information in the computer. Later, you can "cut & paste" to tailor your resume for each specific job. By using a computer, you can avoid expensive typesetting charges.

If you use a computer, don't use an inexpensive daisy wheel or dot matrix printer, even the so-called "letter quality" ones. A laser printer, or an ink jet, works best when preparing the master resume copy for printing. Many print shops have them. Maybe you have access to one at work or a friend.

Rather than having copies made by offset printing, consider having the print shop use a copy machine many of which have different color toners available. Or, simply use an ink jet printer that has different color cartridges printing the number of copies you want. Many office supply stores and printers will sell you a small amount of colored paper. Get enough for your cover letters and the thank you follow up. Matching envelopes are usually available.

If you use a typewriter, make sure the keys are clean and that you have a new ribbon.

Avoid abbreviations as much as possible, though some, such as for states, are acceptable. Employers don't hire people who take shortcuts. Too, some abbreviations are confused with other ones.

When writing your resume, be sure it is readable, even easy to read. If it looks like there is a lot to read, or that it may be hard to read, the employer could well not take the time to read it. Here are some readability pointers:

> 75% of the words should be 8 letters or less
> Sentences/lines should be 12 words or less
> It should have a 7th grade reading level (most newspapers do)
> It should be pleasing to the eye

Push some "hot buttons" when phrasing the components of your resume to motivate the employer to interview you. It is the hot buttons that move the employer to the desired action of interviewing you. Listed below are some employer hot buttons:

Make money Every organization is in operation for the money; even so called non-profit ones. Without money no organization would last long. When possible, your resume should convey how and how much money you have helped firms make in previous employment.

Save money Every organization wants to save money; to reduce costs. Your resume should cite how much money you have saved prior employers and how you did it.

Protect the organization and the boss Show you are a company person with loyalty. Do you practice confidentiality and avoid rumors? Do you follow measures that will assure that the organization continues to survive and assure the boss will remain employed?

Save time That you will begin producing immediately. That you require minimal supervision and only interact with others as needed.

Conserve organization property Have you participated in recycling programs? Have you instituted procedures to reduce waste?

Make the boss's job easier Do you require minimal instruction? Do you seek additional responsibilities?

Customer service Without customers, no organization can survive. Every organization exists to provide goods and services to customers. Are you cordial in all customer interactions? Do you go out of your way to help assure customer satisfaction, even if the customer is wrong?

It has previously been stated that to get a job today you need to sell yourself; and that your resume is a piece of advertising or sales literature. There is an opera called **AIDA** which also happens to be an acronym used for the preparation of advertising and sales literature.

A is for Attention. You want to prepare your resume so that it gets the attention of the employer. It should stand out from the others enticing the employer to read it.

I is for interest. Your resume needs to capture the interest of the employer by the way it looks, the content contained, and how the content is presented.

D is for desire. Your resume should create a desire on the part of the employer to want to interview you by clearly stating through your skills, assets, and accomplishments that you can do the job and get along with others.

A is for action. Your resume should move the employer to the action of inviting you for an interview. The employer has been sold, and at this point is favorably inclined to hire you.

Any resume needs to be understandable. The reader must be able to comprehend exactly what you are stating in your resume. In fact, it should be more than just understandable. The secret to effective communication is to **be <u>not</u> misunderstood**.

Your resume needs to be memorable. It should be prepared so that it will be remembered. More specifically, you want the employer to remember as much of the content as possible. Employers, like anyone else, have short memory spans. Presented information is retained for only a short time. Some experts contend that over 50% is lost after only a few minutes.

Finally, your resume needs to **sell them what they want**. Don't undersell, oversell, or mis-sell. Don't sell a bicycle when they want a car. Don't sell a penthouse suite when they only want a room. Don't sell an alarm clock when they want a loaf of bread.

The Appendix contains a worksheet for you to practice putting your resume together in rough draft form. Don't get discouraged if it doesn't come out right the first time. You will note that the formats vary somewhat, but not that much; they all resemble a piece of advertising or sales literature.

When To Start Your Next Resume

No later than the day you begin your new job is when to start your next *Kick Ass Resume* and your next job search. So don't throw away your worksheets, keep them up-to-date adding information at least monthly, if not weekly or daily. Why? **It is easier to get a job when you have a job!**

Chapter 12

How To Use Your Resume

Congratulations! You have reached the shortest chapter in the book.

There are a variety of ways to use your resume to help sell you. Some are obvious, others are not. Since you have spent a lot of time and effort to prepare an excellent resume, use it for all it's worth. Get as much mileage as you can.

Send, or better yet, take a copy to the employer. Remember, not the personnel department, but the person who will be your supervisor...that's the person who will make the decision...that's the person who is buying what you are selling.

If you have to fill out an application, once it is properly completed, staple a copy of your resume to the top. That way the employer will have to look at your resume before looking at your application. NEVER, NEVER, NEVER write "see resume" on an application leaving it blank! Nor should you ever respond to an application request for information by answering "see resume". You will be viewed as someone who can't follow instructions or comply with a reasonable request.

After you have carefully selected those individuals to use as a reference, being sure you have their permission, give each of them a copy of your resume. That way they will have something to refer to should the employer call. That's better than letting them rely solely on their memory

Take a copy with you to the interview to give to the employer. Resumes do get lost or misplaced. Even better, take 4 or 5 extra copies. You may be interviewed by more than one person, and you want each person to have a copy.

If you are sending a cover letter to an employer in response to an advertisement, a copy of the resume is attached. Additional information on cover letters is presented in the next chapter.

After the interview, you need to follow up with a thank you letter, also a piece of advertising, to the interviewer with a copy of your resume attached. Additional information on thank you letters is presented in Chapter 13.

Part of your job search efforts will involve talking with friends, relatives, acquaintances, and others about your endeavors. This is called networking, and includes informational interviews. Give each one a copy of your resume. You'll reap good dividends; most people get a job in this fashion.

Chapter 13

Cover Letters

Though not always needed, a cover letter is an introduction to, and a good companion of, your resume. Some employers require them. A good cover letter is also a piece of advertising or sales literature like your resume, but the cover letter is more personal. The cover letter permits you to communicate one-on-one with the employer.

Since a cover letter is a personal form of communication, it is always addressed to the employer by name and title. **Never** send a cover letter addressed to: Dear Personnel Manager, To Whom It May Concern, Dear Sir/Madam, Dear Dept. STF, Dear Box holder, or the like.

Use of such an address shows a lack of interest on your part. If you are really interested in the job, you should do whatever is necessary to determine who the cover letter should be sent to...the person who would supervise that position Be sure to have the proper spelling of the person's name and correct title.

The cover letter should be no more than one page in length, keeping it to about four hard hitting paragraphs. Do not repeat too many phrases of information contained in the resume, but what is said needs to entice the employer to read the resume.

The first sentence needs to be a grabber, an attention getter. Persuade the employer to keep reading. The first sentence can make the difference.

Another grabber is a PS. Many times the PS is read before the letter, so it needs to be a strong sales feature just like the opening sentence. Not to minimize the importance of the rest of the cover letter, the first sentence and the PS should be strong enough to encourage the reading of your resume even if the majority of the letter is not read nor long remembered.

The use of bullets, underlining, all capital letters, or boldface type can, and should, be used in parts of the letter for emphasis drawing the reader's attention to those facts so noted. Avoid the over-use of "I". Use it no more than three times in a four paragraph letter.

As with your resume, plan to take the time to do your cover letter right, and this includes careful editing. Be sure it is crisp and clearly readable being presented on paper that matches your resume preferably.

The cover letter, as the resume, needs to be targeted to a specific job with a specific organization. If you are seeking a position as a warehouse forklift operator, say so telling the reasons why you would be an asset to the organization. Tell the employer the benefits that would be provided in hiring you. Remember, it should be addressed to the warehouse manager by name.

Many employers don't like to interview and go through the hiring process because they feel they would be making a bad decision that could reflect negatively on them. Help them make the decision by convincing them in the cover letter that they will be making a good decision in hiring you; a decision that will reflect positively in your favor.

In a sales situation, which you are in, a good sales person helps the buyer make a decision. Instead of letting the employer decide whether to contact you, state in your cover letter that you will initiate that contact. Simply state in the last paragraph of your letter that you will call on a specific day at a specific time.

A traditional business letter format is acceptable to use in your cover letter. That is:

Date

Name
Title
Company
Address

Salutation:

Opening paragraph and grabber.

Second paragraph

* A few hard-hitting bulleted items
*
*
*
*

Closing paragraph

Ending

Signature

Name
Address
Phone

PS

The address and phone number beneath the signature is primarily used only when that information is not on a letterhead. Don't forget to sign the cover letter, preferably with your first name only, or whatever it is you like to be called. You are trying to make the cover letter personable, but it is recommended you avoid nicknames such as "Bullet", "Shorty", and "Echo".

Another cover letter format to consider has no salutation with the date and address near the end. This permits having a strong attention getter or grabber at the very beginning. This format is similar to that used by many direct marketing firms. It offers the advantage of having your cover letter (and resume) stand out from the rest.

Practice writing a cover letter on the worksheet in the Appendix drawing information from the skills, assets, and accomplishments worksheets already completed.

Chapter 14

Thank You Letters

Sending a simple thank you letter is the most over-looked part of a job search by most job seekers. Bad move. It can mean the difference between getting the job or not! While a letter is best, at least send a note, mailgram, FAX, or E-mail.

The thank you letter is yet another opportunity to sell yourself for the job. Like the resume and cover letter, it should be viewed as a piece of advertising or sales literature. As the cover letter, the thank you letter is a one-on-one personal communication with the employer. In it re-emphasize that you can do the job and fit in.

Include items discussed during the interview. This shows you were attentive and take your job search seriously. Cite at least one, if not two or three, important topics the employer and you covered during the interview. Point out the benefits the employer would gain by hiring you. Present additional sales features if needed. If you had trouble answering a question, or there was some information not covered, now is the time to rectify it.

Do not draw attention to any negative aspect of the interview.

Carefully phrase your thank you letter; this is not the time for haste. Be sure it sells you in the best light possible. It's not unusual to have six or seven drafts before the letter is just right. Don't forget to edit for misspelled words and poor grammar.

The thank you letter should be addressed to the person, by title, who interviewed you. If you were in a multiple interview, send a thank you letter to each person who interviewed you, or at least send a copy of the original. A copy of your resume should be attached to a thank you letter.

Even if you were rejected for the job during the interview, you still need to send a thank you letter. This is not the time to burn bridges. Leave the door open; perhaps there will soon be another opening with the organization. Sometimes, that future opening is better than the one for which you originally interviewed.

Thank you letters should be typed (handwritten is okay if your penmanship is good) on the same paper as your resume and cover letter. This provides continuity helping the employer relate to all three documents.

It is recommended that the thank you letter be hand-delivered to the person who interviewed you. Mail does get lost or delivered late. Take it to the employer promptly, no more than 24 hours after the interview. If you were interviewed in the morning, deliver it the same afternoon. If you were interviewed in the afternoon, be there with the thank you letter when the organization opens for business the following morning. This tactic has been successfully used by hundreds of job seekers.

Examples of the power of the hand-delivered thank you letter:

One person, after much cajoling, hand-delivered the thank letter and was offered the job on the spot.

Another, whom the employer said interviewed like a "lump", hand-delivered the thank you letter also being hired immediately.

A favorite anecdote about hand-delivered thank you letters really demonstrates their power. The job seeker was 20 minutes late for the interview, and swore afterwards in tears, that the job was lost because of it. Normally, she would be right. But, she hand-delivered the thank you letter first thing the next morning. She left the employer's office in less than an hour with a job that paid $7,500 more than her last one.

In one case, there were three people more qualified than another job seeker, and the three interviewed better. However, he got the job by providing a thank you letter which the others neglected to do.

Thank you letters are not reserved for just following up an interview, nor just for the employer. Other uses:

+ People you select for references

+ Those who provide you with job leads

+ To confirm an invitation to interview

+ To confirm acceptance of the job, salary, and starting date

+ Don't overlook the secretary or receptionist

When preparing a thank you letter, follow the same concepts in preparing a cover letter and your resume.

Chapter 15

Job Search Tips

Looking for a job, is a job. It is hard work, and very competitive. You need to treat your job search efforts the same way you would treat a job. Spend at least 40 hours each week if you are unemployed, and 20 hours if you are working. This is not to suggest that the entire time is devoted to "pounding the pavement".

Time spent completing the worksheets counts. So does time spent reading this book. Read some good job search books as part of your efforts. Many books have been written on the topic, some excellent, some good, and some aren't worth the time. And frankly, some contain poor advice.

I have been recommending *What Color Is Your Parachute* (updated every year) by Richard Bolles since 1974, and still do. He also conducts seminars and has a website.

A successful job search begins by getting rid of any garbage you may have and working through the grieving process. You must be in the right frame of mind, and the key word is "positive". There is a job out there for you.

In business management there is an old axiom: "plan your work, and work your plan." The same holds true for job search. Look at it as a sales and marketing campaign. You are selling and marketing yourself to get a job. You need a plan of attack that can be placed on a calendar of eight hour days of five or six days each week. This helps having an organized job search campaign.

The job search is organized around those things that need to be accomplished: networking, resume preparation, interviews, using the telephone to tap into the hidden job market, writing cover letters and thank you letters, filling out applications, reading the classified help wanted advertisements, touching base with job service and employment agencies, developing a list of interview questions you may be asked and answering them, preparing a list of questions to ask the employer, and researching the organizations.

That's a lot of things to accomplish. Devoting three hours to each, you have already allotted 36 hours of time. Add travel and you are probably over 40 hours a week. It's no wonder that getting a job is a full time job.

However, you cannot get organized until you have decided what the main goal is. The goal is just not just any job, but the kind of job you want. A job you will be happy doing. And this is your first decision. If you haven't decided on the right job, go back and read the chapter, ***Deciding What You Want To Do***.

Set up a job search "office space" for yourself. You will need a phone, desk or table, comfortable chair computer and/or typewriter, paper, pens and pencils, markers or highlighters, stapler, envelopes, stamps, index cards, file folders, and the like. The work space needs to be free from distractions. No radio or television. Away from the fridge. Do not let family or friends interrupt your important job search tasks unless it is related or an emergency.

Establish goals or objectives: Two personal networking contacts, seventeen phone contacts, and one interview each day.

When looking for a job, you need to use all of the options available: newspaper classifieds, employment agencies, Job Service, cold calling, organization "job hotlines", and the Internet. There are even books on job hunting just on the Internet. Some methods are more effective than others. This is called the open job market.

The most effective method is to tap into the hidden job market. The open job market probably accounts for only 10% of the jobs available at any given time, while the rest are in the hidden job market.

It is interesting to note that 90% of all job seekers devote their efforts solely to the open job market. That means that 90% of the people are competing for 10% of the jobs. Highly competitive. Improve your chances by being part of the 10% of the people looking for the 90% of the jobs in the hidden job market.

Networking is the most effective way to tap into the hidden job market. Networking should not be mysterious or frightening; it is merely talking with people. Presenting yourself. Asking questions. Usually just plain conversation.

It is easy to begin your networking efforts. First talk with relatives, then friends. Let them know you are looking for a job, and what kind. Don't just ask who they know who has a job opening, or who's hiring. Ask them who they know that could use your talents. Most jobs are filled in this manner; people talking with people.

You will face rejection; learn to accept it. Rejection does not mean you are a bad person. When making phone contacts, you may experience "no" 30 or more times before you get a "yes". Each "no" gets you closer to that "yes".

Most jobs are with small organizations that probably have fewer than 50 employees, so be sure not to overlook them.

If you meet 50% or more of the requirements for a job, go after it. The bottom line is that employers hire you because they like you. The hiring process is emotional, not logical. It is your responsibility to initiate the liking.

Avoid sending lots of organizations unsolicited generic resumes. The response rate is usually very poor. This job hunting method is like direct mail advertising. Those that are in direct mail advertising are usually satisfied with a 1% - 3% response rate, some even less. With a 1% response rate, you would have to send out 100 resumes to get just one reply, which probably would be, "Sorry, we don't have any openings at this time."

The hiring process is a buying/selling process. A good sales person (you) must know the product being sold (you) inside out. Know your sales features: Skills, assets, and accomplishments. Then, as part of your sales efforts, prepare a *Kick Ass Resume* !

Chapter 16

The Internet

The Internet, often referred to as simply the "Net", is also known as Cyberspace, The Information Superhighway, and the World Wide Web (WWW); let's you conduct almost all portions of your job search "on line". It can let you conduct your job search more effectively, efficiently, and economically...it can make it much easier. It is the fastest growing system of human communication in history, and is the world's largest information resource.

Using your computer, a friend's, or the library's with a modem and an Internet Service Provider you can plug into the Net to do or get:

Career exploration	Vocational profiling	Career counseling
Skills analysis	Wage information	Vocational assessment
Labor market statistics	Job listings	Job matching
Job search tips /advice	Career analysis	PLUS MUCH MORE !

It is possible to send your resume to employers over the Net by e-mail, conduct preliminary interviews by e-mail or "chat", and send a thank you follow up letter.

If the organization has a Net presence (and a several million do), you can gather a wealth of background information on a variety of areas by visiting their web site. You can learn about the operation. You can gain knowledge of their products and services. You can get contact names including titles. You can get pertinent news about what's going on. Often the site will list employment opportunities and how to make application. Job descriptions are often available. There are many search engines such as Google, Lycos, AltaVista, HotBot, and Yahoo! that can help you determine if the organization has a web site and how to access it.

Another source for organizational information, and one of the best sites, is Yahoo!'s finance site where a wealth of knowledge can be gleaned. You can learn of the firm's financial condition. How many shares of stock trade on an average day. A rating of management effectiveness. What others think. Quite often there is a link to the web site of a specific organization you are researching. The list is almost endless.

An excellent site (and it is a governmental one) is America's Job Bank at www.jobbankinfo.org which is visited more than a half billion times each year. It contains jobs listed with all the Job Service offices in the nation. Here you can get leads for specific types of jobs. You can even narrow your search to each of the 50 states. You can get wage and salary information. Job search tips and advice are available to you. There is even one on preparing your resume for the Internet, by Margaret F. Dikel.

Anyone searching for a job and preparing **Kick Ass Resumes** needs to know about salary. *Salary.com* will assist you in this facet providing information based on title, level and location.

Other web sites well worth checking out are Career Mosaic, CareerPath and Career Magazine, Career Builder, Job.Com, Jobhunt.org, and Monster to name just a few of the many. There are many, many more, and you should avail yourself of them.

There are also several books on using the Net in your job search efforts. Many are available in most bookstores or can be quickly ordered for you. Your local library is also a source to consider.

A Few Words Of Caution

You need to be discreet when using the Net in your job search efforts, especially if you are currently employed since it could cost you your job if your boss discovered you are looking for another position. The Net is public, and your boss could find your resume should you post it.

Also, your organization may have computer "watch dogs"; so be very cautious about using your computer at work to conduct job search activities. Even though you may try to cover up all traces, there are a variety of internal components of a computer that provide a pretty accurate map of where you have been and what you have been doing.

EXTREME CAUTION

Do not, repeat DO NOT give a hiring authority any personal internet and telecommunication sources including *facebook, myspace, youtube, twitter, Email address OR cell phone* containing what an employer would consider inappropriate or offensive information. Employers are conservative and don't like shocking information.

If need be, change your cell phone voice mail greeting, or even purchase a "throw away" cell phone using it specifically for job search. Get a separate Email account related solely to your job search. And be sure the cell phone is turned off during the interview!

Afterword

This book is not finished, and never will be. It will be revised and updated as things change, and they always do.

You can be part of that change.

Simply write to me with your suggestions for content improvement. Send me copies of your resume, cover letter, and thank you letters for possible inclusion in the next edition. (Your name, address, and phone number will be disguised).

If you have any amusing anecdotes concerning resumes or other parts of job search, please pass those along also for inclusion in revised editions of *Kick Ass Resumes*.

Good luck to you in all parts of your job search efforts. Remember the scout motto: "be prepared". Preparation is a vital key. Now, go *Kick Ass* !

William (Bill) McClintic
kickresume@hotmail.com

APPENDIX

Worksheets:

Experiences
Skills
Assets
Accomplishments
Ideal Job Description
What Employers Want
Typical Interview Questions
Putting It Together
Cover Letter Preparation

WORKSHEET 1

EXPERIENCES

Put these in a computer file and keep up-to-date. Number each one.

1. Doing what was asked (example)

2.

4.

2. Getting along with others

3.

5.

Worksheet 2

Skills

On this worksheet, which will be the foundation of each resume, list all the skills you possess creating a word picture to accurately convey them to an employer. Skills are a most important thing that you can convey to the employer, for it is skills that permit a person to do the job that needs to be done.

If you have not used a skill or ability in quite some time, it still belongs on the worksheet. It may be helpful to refer to your completed worksheet on experiences. You can then think separately about each writing down the skills used. If you need some help in this area you may want to discuss it with others. Another good place to turn is the library. Most will have the *Occupational Outlook Handbook*, old copies of the *Dictionary of Occupational Titles*, and similar publications in which skills are discussed.

Even skills that are not related to a job you have held should be on the worksheet. Coaching little league activities involves supervisory and management skills. Serving as a volunteer church secretary requires skills that can be listed. Creating props for a school play involves skills to be listed. Don't forget hobbies. An amateur photographer operates equipment and uses composition.

Use the action words when creating a word picture of your skills. Avoid complete sentences; this helps create action and excitement. Remember, your resume is a piece of advertising or sales literature, not an English composition.

Avoid using pronouns such as: I, me, he, hers, we, ours, you and your.

The information on the completed worksheet will be used not only for the resume, but also writing the cover letter, during the interview, and in composing the thank you and follow up letters. It will also be used in preparing a letter of acceptance. After completion, enter them into a computer file and keep up-to-date.

Skill

Skill

Skill

Skill

Skill

Skill

Worksheet 3
Assets Identification
Make additional copies of this blank worksheet as needed.

Asset

Asset

Asset

Asset

Asset

Asset

Worksheet 4
Accomplishments Identification

Make as many copies of this blank worksheet as needed.

*

*

*

*

*

*

Worksheet 5

Ideal Job Description

      When preparing your ideal job description, rank order your skills, assets, and accomplishments writing the most important one first by simply referring back to your already completed worksheets. Don't put a title on it until you determine what type of job it fits. Because there are jobs that are quite similar in nature, it is recommended that you develop 4 or 5 ideal job descriptions. For example, there are many similarities between a machinist and a tool & die maker.

Title:

Skills:

1.

2.

3.

4.

5.

6.

7.

8.

9.

10.

Assets:

1.

2.

3.

4.

5.

6.

7.

8.

9.

10.

Accomplishments:

1.

2.

3.

4.

5.

6.

7.

8.

9.

10.

Comments (Note any other pertinent information below)

Worksheet 6

What Employers Want

    This worksheet should be completed to fine tune your skills, assets, and accomplishments placing them in the order being sought by the employer. Make additional copies as needed for your personal use.

Company: **Position:**

Address:

City: **State:**   **Zip:**

Contact:

Phone: **FAX:**   **e-mail:**

Job:

Organization:

Boss:

Comments:

Worksheet 7
Typical Interview Questions

Typical interview questions asked by employers often indicate what employers are looking for and that information can be transferred to your worksheets, cover letter and resume. Samples are below with space to draft your answers. In addition, you should expand the list to at least 40 questions you think the employer needs answered including 10 that you "hope to God aren't asked", because they probably will be. You answers should focus solely in relationship to the specific job applied for and your background that has prepared you for it. Fine tune your answers phrasing the them as positively as possible, and where possible, include versions of them as part of your resume and letters.

"Tell me about yourself" is the most frequently raised topic by an employer during an interview, most often being the first. Do not waste the employer's time by starting with where you were born, where you went to elementary school, and so b-o-r-i-n-g on. It is better to begin, "I began preparing for this position by taking the classes necessary to provide a good foundation, then applying the concepts learned in my first job as a ....." Keep your response brief and to the point.

Tell me about yourself.

Why should I hire you?

Why do you want to work here?

Why do you want this job?

What are your three biggest accomplishments

How would others describe you?

What 3 skills do you use the most?

What has prepared you for this job?

What are your 3 major assets?

How would your last supervisor describe you?

How do you get along with others?

Why do (did) you want to leave your current position?

If you had it to do over again, what would you change?

Who did you interact with on your last job?

What was your favorite subject in school?

What do (did) you like least about your job?

Who is your favorite person?

How many days did you miss from work in the last year?

How did you rate on your last performance evaluation?

What are (were) your duties and responsibilities?

Why are you seeking another job?

Who has been the major influence in your life and why?

What do (did) you like most about your job?

What is (was) the biggest job crisis and how did you handle it?

Worksheet 8

Putting It Together

SUMMARY:

ACCOMPLISHMENTS:
 *
 *
 *
 *
 *
 *
 *
 *

SKILLS:
 =
 =
 =
 =
 =
 =
 =
 =

ASSETS:

+
+
+
+
+
+
+

GRABBER:

Worksheet 9
Letter Preparation

(Date)

(Name)
(Title)
(Organization)
(Address)
(City, State, Zip)

(Salutation)

    (Grabber)

    (Content Paragraph)

    *
    *
    *
    *
    *

(Closing Paragraph)

              Cordially,

PS

A

Accelerate
Accept
Account
Achieve
Act
Activate
Acquire
Adapt
Administer
Adopt
Address
Advance
Advise
Alert
Alter
Appraise
Apprise
Approve
Analyze
Answer
Anticipate
Apply
Appoint
Arbitrate
Arrange
Ascertain
Assess
Assemble
Assist
Attain
Audit
Avoid

B

Back
Balance
Bargain
Base
Begin
Bolster
Boost
Break
Bring
Budget
Build
Buy

C

Calculate
Centralize
Certify
Chart
Check
Choose
Cite
Classify
Coach
Collaborate
Collect
Combine
Compile
Complete
Compose
Compute
Communicate
Conceive

Construct
Control
Coordinate
Copy
Correct
Craft
Create
Counsel
Curtail
Cut

D

Decentralize
Decide
Decorate
Decrease
Deduce
Define
Delegate
Deliver
Demonstrate
Design
Detail
Detect
Determine
Develop
Devise
Diagnose
Dig
Direct
Discover
Discuss
Dispense
Display

Action Words

Disprove
Dissect
Distribute
Double
Dramatize
Draw
Drive

E

Earn
Edit
Educate
Effect
Elevate
Embody
Embrace
Employ
Empower
Enforce
Engage
Enhance
Enlarge
Enlighten
Enlist
Ensue
Ensure
Entertain
Entitle
Enumerate
Erase
Erect
Establish
Evaluate
Evolve

Examine
Execute
Expand
Expedite
Expend
Experiment
Explain
Express
Extract

F

Fabricate
Facilitate
Figure
File
Fill
Finalize
Finance
Find
Finish
Fix
Flourish
Fly
Float
Follow
Forecast
Form
Formulate
Found
Frame
Fulfill
Furnish

G

Gain
Gather
Gauge
Generate
Get
Give
Govern
Grant
Gratify
Group
Guide

H

Hail
Halt
Harden
Handle
Harmonize
Have
Head
Heighten
Help
Hire
Hold
Honor

I

Identify
Illustrate
Imagine
Implement

Improve
Improvise
Increase
Influence
Inform
Initiate
Innovate
Inspect
Inspire
Install
Institute
Insure
Integrate
Interchange
Interpret
Interview
Introduce
Instruct
Invent
Inventory
Investigate

J

Jibe
Job
Join
Judge
Justify
Jump
Juxtapose

K

Keep

Key
Kick
Kindle
Kiss
Knead
Knit
Know

L

Last
Laud
Laugh
Launch
Lead
Learn
Lecture
Level
Lift
Light
Like
Line
Listen
Live
Load
Loan
Locate
Log
Loose
Lose
Love
Lower

M

Maintain
Magnify
Manage
Manipulate
Manufacture
Make
Mark
Market
Master
Match
Mean
Measure
Mediate
Meet
Memorize
Mend
Mention
Mentor
Minimize
Minister
Mitigate
Model
Moderate
Modernize
Modify
Monitor
Motivate
Move

N

Name
Narrate
Narrow
Naturalize

Action Words

Navigate
Necessitate
Need
Negate
Negotiate
Neutralize
Nip
Nominate
Normalize
Note
Notify
Nourish
Nullify
Number
Numerate
Nurture

O

Obey
Object
Oblige
Observe
Obtain
Offer
Open
Operate
Oppose
Order
Organize
Oversee

P

Package

Paint
Participate
Pass
Perceive
Perform
Persuade
Photograph
Pilot
Pinpoint
Pioneer
Plan
Play
Prepare
Prescribe
Present
Prevent
Print
Process
Procure
Produce
Program
Project
Promote
Proofread
Propose
Protect
Prove
Provide
Publicize
Publish
Purchase

Q

Qualify

Quantify
Quell
Quench
Query
Question
Quiet
Quit
Quote

R

Raise
Read
Realize
Reason
Receive
Recommend
Record
Recruit
Redesign
Refer
Rehabilitate
Regulate
Reinforce
Reject
Relate
Remember
Render
Reorganize
Repair
Report
Represent
Research
Resolve
Respond

Restore
Retrieve
Reveal
Revamp
Reverse
Review
Revise
Revitalize
Reward
Rise
Risk
Rival
Role-play
Rotate
Rouse
Run

S

Satisfy
Save
Schedule
Seek
Select
Sell
Sense
Separate
Serve
Service
Set
Settle
Sew
Shape
Share

Ship
Show
Simplify
Sketch
Solve
Sort
Spark
Spearhead
Specify
Staff
Standardize
Start
State
Stimulate
Streamline
Strengthen
Stress
Structure
Study
Style
Substantiate
Succeed
Summarize
Supervise
Support
Survey
Systematize

T

Tabulate
Take
Teach
Tell
Tend

Terminate
Temporize
Test
Testify
Theorize
Think
Tie
Tighten
Tolerate
Toss
Total
Touch
Toughen
Trace
Track
Trade
Train
Transcribe
Transform
Translate
Transmit
Transpire
Trim
Triple
Tutor
Type

U

Umpire
Undergo
Understand
Undertake
Unify
Unite

Action Words

Unravel
Upgrade
Urge
Use
Utter
Utilize

V

Vacate
Validate
Value
Vary
Vend
Vent
Verbalize
Verge
Verify
Vest
Vie
View
Vindicate
Visit
Visualize
Vivify
Vocalize
Voice
Void
Volunteer
Vote
Vouch
Vow

W

Watch
Wear
Weather
Weave
Weed
Weigh
Widen
Wield
Win
Withdraw
Withstand
Witness Work
Wrap
Wrench
Write

XYZ

I couldn't find any
for these.

A

Accommodation
Accordance
Accountable
Adjustable
Affability
Allegiance
Ambition
Approachable
Assertiveness
Assurance
Astuteness
Attendance
Attentiveness

B

Balance
Behavior
Belief
Beneficiation
Benevolent
Bi-lingual
Boldness
Broadminded

C

Calmness
Candid
Candor
Careful
Character
Charitable

Charm
Cheerfulness
Civility
Cogent
Coherent
Collegial
Commendability
Comportment
Composure
Concentration
Conceptualize
Concordant
Conduct
Confident
Confident
Confidentiality
Conform
Congenial
Conscience
Conscientious
Conscionable
Considerate
Constitution
Constructive
Contemplative
Content
Conversant
Cool-headed
Cope
Cordial
Counsel
Creed
Curiosity

D

Dauntless
Decent
Decisive
Dedication
Deliberate
Demeanor
Deportment
Determination
Dignified
Dialectic
Diligent
Diplomatic
Direct
Discerning
Discernment
Discreet
Disposition
Dogged
Durable

E

Earnest
Easygoing
Economical
Efficient
Elocution
Eloquent
Empathetic
Endurance
Enterprising
Entertaining
Enthusiastic
Energetic
Equable

Asset Words

Equanimity
Equitable
Erudite
Esprit
Esteem
Ethical
Even-tempered
Expressive

F

Facilitative
Far-sighted
Fidelity
Flexible
Fluent
Focused
Fortitude
Frank
Friendliness
Frugal

G

Generosity
Geniality
Genteel
Gentility
Good-humored
Good-natured
Good-tempered
Goodness
Graciousness
Gumption

H

Harmonious
Honest
Honorable
Humane
Humorousness

I

Impartial
Incisive
Industrious
Ingenuous
Ingratiable
Integrity
Intellectual
Intelligent
Intuitive

J

Jocular
Jocund
Jolly
Jovial
Judgment
Judicious
Justness

K

Kind
Kindly

Knowledgeable

L

Learned
Level-headed
Likable
Lively
Logical
Loyalty

M

Matter-of-fact
Maturity
Meditative
Memory
Merry
Methodical
Mien
Mindful
Mirthful
Moderate
Modest
Moral
Motivated

N

Neat
Negotiator
Neighborly
Nonpareil
Notable
Noteworthy

O

Objective
Observant
Open-minded
Optimistic
Organized

P

Painstaking
Patient
Perceptive
Perseverance
Persistent
Personable
Perspicacious
Persuasive
Pleasant
Pleasing
Pluck
Polite
Popular
Positive
Practical
Precise
Proactive
Probity
Productive
Proficient
Progressive
Prompt
Prospective
Prudent

Q

Qualified

R

Rational
Realistic
Reasonable
Receptive
Rectitude
Reliable
Reliant
Reputable
Resolute
Respectable
Respectful
Responsible
Retentive
Risk-taking

S

Sagacious
Sane
Sapient
Scholarly
Sedate
Self-command
Self-conscious
Self-control
Self-esteem
Self-motivated
Self-respect

Sensibility
Sentient
Serenity
Skillful
Sociable
Soundness
Spirituality
Spontaneous
Spunk
Stately
Steadfast
Steady
Strong
Studious
Subjective
Successful
Supportive
Systematic

T

Tactful
Teachable
Temperament
Tenacity
Thinking
Thorough
Thoughtful
Thrifty
Timely
Tranquil
Transactive
Trustworthy

Asset Words

U

Understanding
Undeterred
Upright
Urbane

V

Veracious
Vibrant
Vigilance
Vigorous
Virtuous
Vivacious
Volubility

W

Well-being
Well-mannered
Wholesome
Wisdom
Wise
Wistful
Wit
Work-ethic

XYZ

None found

| 10257 Calibri | Duncan, YO 95051 | 555-912-1011 |

People want Les Hassle in customer service!

You can capitalize on my name and have the best customer service at the same time. In addition to the skills and assets contained in the attached resume, I also:
* Reduced returns to a mere 1/2%
* Improved response time to under a brief minute
* Initiated a customer satisfaction survey

Not only will the job get done (and correctly) you may rest assured that I will fit into the organization quite well as evidenced by:
* Staff retention program development
* Cited twice as "employee of the year"
* Outstanding performance evaluations

Regards,

Mr. Lee Eyea   September 10, 2010
Coca Cola Bottlers

A Customer Is A Terrible Thing To Lose

```
┌─────────────────────────────────────────────────────────────────┐
│                        Ralph S. Weird                             │
│   317 E. Grant * Denver, CO 80220                      303-555-    │
│                            1212                                    │
└─────────────────────────────────────────────────────────────────┘
```

Mr. Sam Sung   May 10, 2010
Sing, Sing, Sing Song

   Thank you for interviewing me this morning for the position of
Special Delivery Driver for your firm. I am confident that my skills fit your
needs quite well.

   = Strict compliance with DOT regulations
   = Maintain accurate records and logs
   = Utilize preventive maintenance
   = Organize cargo for optimum load capacity

   Your sense of humor seems to coincide with my own, and you can
rely on me for timely completion of assigned tasks. As mentioned, my
background includes being awarded a safe driving certificate.

   I can report to work the morning of the 17th unless the first of the
month fits your calendar needs better.

Sincerely,


```
┌─────────────────────────────────────────────────────────────────┐
│                  While Others Talk...I Deliver                    │
└─────────────────────────────────────────────────────────────────┘
```

Steven M. Gregg - 111 Front St. - Oakes, OH 68357	343-555-1212

Mr. Paul Graham   February 3, 2009
Haveahurtin Construction

Good afternoon,

The purpose of this letter, Paul, is to confirm my acceptance of the Project Manager position with Haveahurtin Construction offered me this morning; I look forward to being part of your team utilizing my skills to the best extent possible while learning much from you. The starting salary of $57,000 with a 3 month review is acceptable.

I also acknowledge that a 3 week paid vacation is available after the completion of 9 months employment and that while the company pays all of the life insurance premium that health insurance premiums are split 50/50.

Looking forward to a long term mutually beneficial working relationship that begins the 18th, I remain

Sincerely,

Dedicated to getting the job done right...the first time

GINA SPRATT

| 8 No. Lean * Plate, TX 04913 | 947- 555-1212 |

Jack Fat   October 21, 1990

Seareeous, PLC

This letter is to confirm our interview scheduled for tomorrow morning at 9:30 concerning the position of Sales Development Manager with your firm. I have attached a copy of my resume for your records. Please note that my background includes:

= Developing sales contests and sales incentive programs

= Writing sales manuals

= Successful sales using feature/benefit approach

= Training others to achieve sales goals

Not only do I possess the skills needed to perform all assigned duties and responsibilities, but also the necessary human interaction abilities to be an asset to the organization.

Regards,

Act as organization ambassador to the community

STEVEN M. GREGG   *   111 Front St.   *   Oakes, Ohio 68357   *   343-555-1212

SUMMARY : Increasingly responsible positions in residential and commercial construction and maintenance from single family dwelling to high-rise office buildings including shopping centers and manufacturing facilities.

ACCOMPLISHMENTS :
+ Awarded promotion to construction office manager for manufacturing plant
+ Selected to maintain inventory control on thousands of construction items
+ Chosen to monitor and control all employee time records for payroll
+ Appointed to log employee time analysis for proper construction component costing
+ Promoted to supervise crew of 10 cement finishers for multi-tier parking garage
+ Spearheaded creation of building maintenance business for over 2,000 accounts
+ Cited for completing $4 million office building 3% under budget and 11 days early
+ Named employee of the month 3 times in 2 years

SKILLS :
= Purchase construction and maintenance equipment, tools, and supplies
= Utilize just in time delivery to avoid over stocked inventory tying up money resources
= Prepare bills of material from architectural print take offs
= Supervise activities of others and evaluate performance
= Develop detailed construction and maintenance bids of time and material
= Submit appropriate reports as required
= Maintain OSHA and HAZMAT records in proper formats
= Conduct employee health & safety training

ASSETS:
* Effectively communicate with construction laborers, engineers, and executives
* Honest in all interactions with others
* Self starter requiring minimal supervision
* Get along with people of diverse backgrounds
* Exercise calm, mature judgment
* Sense of humor that attracts others
* Strive for 2-way confidence and respect
* Foster teamwork environment conducive to increased productivity

Dedicated to getting the job done right...the first time

132

RALPH S. WEIRD

317 East Grant * Denver, CO 80220   303-555-1212

SUMMARY: Experienced, over-the-road, DOT certified commercial vehicle driver specializing in 18 wheeler.

ACCOMPLISHMENTS:
* Reduced delivery time 20% using non-peak times and routes
* Awarded safe driving certificate for 3 years with no accidents
* Established preventive maintenance program that saved $57,000 annually
* Won regiment driving skills contest
* Graduated 3rd of 74 from Acme Truck Driving School
* State champion high school engine trouble shooting contest
* Received certificate of completion US Army medium vehicle driving course

SKILLS:

= Strict compliance with DOT regulations
= Operate delivery vans, passenger busses, and 18 wheel semi-trucks
= HAZMAT trained and certified taking yearly refresher class
= Maintain accurate log book and other records
= Utilize preventive maintenance techniques for all vehicle components
= Supervise the activity of others and evaluate performance
= Organize cargo for optimum cube load capacity

ASSETS:

+ Exercise calm mature judgment in all situations
+ Utilize patience in getting along with others
+ Cheerful disposition underscored by good sense of humor
+ Reliable dependability for timely completion of assigned tasks
+ Honest integrity in all dealings
+ Communicate well both written and oral
+ Loyal to organization and supervisor

While Others Talk,,,I Deliver

C. JANE RUN 1231 Russet Camden, GA 97131   517-888-212

SUMMARY: Creative internal and external multi-media experience for business and education organizations with an emphasis on cost efficient timely effectiveness possessing a proven background in product promotion.

EXPERIENCE:

June, 1996 - Present
Sales Promotion Director; Pulp Paper Products Co.; Camden, GA

* Chosen to develop, edit, and publish internal and external monthly newsletters
* Assigned responsibility for preparation of all news releases
* Selected to prepare technical writing copy for industry publications
* Cited for creativity in communications, design, and promotion
* Recognized for initiating **"Product Of The Month"** sales campaign increasing revenue 21%

January, 1994 - June, 1996
Media Center Assistant Director; Keller College; Quintner, TX

* Appointed to develop computer Internet World Wide Web site
* Produced annual college catalog bulletin 16% under assigned budget
* Wrote script for freshman orientation slide show presentation
* Given responsibility for creating exhibit for use by admissions in student recruiting
* Promoted to supervise staff of 3

SKILLS:	ASSETS:
= Prepare copy in an easily understood manner	+ Project professional image
= Utilize JAVA in computer Web site development	+ Motivated self-starter
= Operate variety of multi-media equipment	+ Require little supervision
= Computer literate using Macintosh	+ Patience in interactions with others
= Adept in catalog layout formats	+ Merit confidence and respect
= Estimate printing costs within 5% of actual	+ Dedicated integrity in all situations
= Develop targeted sales efforts	+ Proven "leadership by example"
= Staff performance evaluation	+ Foster teamwork atmosphere

Get along well with others of all levels

Kick Ass & Chronological combination

GINA SPRATT

8 No. Lean * Plate, TX 04913   976-555-1212

SUMMARY: Business management background with proven experience in advertising, human resources, sales, and training specializing in small organizations requiring multi-talented staff.

ADVERTISING:
- = Utilize publicity and public relations to stretch promotional budget dollars
- = Prepare variety of effective media campaigns
- = Completed 4 color 150 page catalogue 17% under assigned budget
- = Cited for creativity in design and color selection
- = Professionally interact with artists, photographers, and others

HUMAN RELATIONS:
- = Assigned responsibility for all personnel functions for employee staff of 35
- = Developed complete human resources program initiating implementation
- = Chosen to teach **Personnel Management** at local college
- = Prepared ADA compliant job descriptions for all organizational positions
- = Wrote employee handbook setting forth policy, procedures, rules, and regulations

SALES:
- = Developed sales contests and sales incentive programs
- = Selected to write sales manual for institutional hard goods
- = Successfully sold tangibles and intangibles using **feature - benefit** approach
- = Appointed to train new and existing sales staff
- = Awarded bonus for outstanding sales performance of 91% closure rate

TRAINING:
- = Rated as very dynamic trainer by 98% of trainees
- = Designed pre-test/post-test methods for measuring training program effectiveness
- = Performance of those trained above expected levels
- = Use variety of training techniques and aids to assist in content retention
- = Established successful employee cross-training program

Act as organization ambassador to the community

135

ROBERT FISHER

455 W. Highland, Yuma, AZ 76101   **976-505-9797**

SUMMARY: Food service management experience involving preparation, service, sales, catering, and banquets with strengths in cost control, menu planning, staffing, and supervision.

ACHIEVEMENTS:
  * Cited by national food operation organization for:
       Lowest labor cost (44%) through strategic staff scheduling
       Lowest food cost (37%) by adherence to portion control
       Lowest beverage cost (19%) due to inventory monitoring and security
  * Consistently passed rigid health department inspections with very high ratings
  * Initiated continuous employee training program
  * Selected to manage 7 departments and 80 employees
  * Established employee decision making participation by committee initiation
  * Noted for continuous excellent meal quality through recipe adherence

---

ABILITIES:
  = Prepare monthly, quarterly, and yearly budget forecasts
  = Establish/maintain inventory control of beverages, equipment, food items, supplies
  = Conduct daily staff meetings to assure communication of "what's going on"
  = Train employees in tasks to be performed with standards to be met
  = Devise staff schedules for proper coverage
  = Purchase all items needed for operations and customer satisfaction of choices
  = Monitor time sheets and payroll for accuracy
  = Inspect total facility each day for meeting health and safety guidelines
  = Contact organizations for meeting and catering events to maximize facility usage
  = Develop advertising and promotional campaigns

ASSETS:
  + Create atmosphere conducive to teamwork increasing staff job satisfaction
  + Cheerful disposition that puts others at ease
  + Exercise calm patience in all interactions
  + Practice "open door" policy in employee relations
  + Provide leadership supervision by setting example
  + Adhere to honesty in all situations
  + Get along well with others by treating each individual with respect

---

136

Walter Scott - 2983 Convoy - Fairplay, GA 99907   976 - 303 - 1212

SUMMARY: Business and sales management experience including direction of daily operations, accounting, advertising, human resources, marketing, sales, payroll, proposal/bid preparation, public relations, and staff training.

ACHIEVEMENTS:
* Hired to direct all aspects of small business venture marketing products nationwide
* Assigned responsibility for all accounting and financial operations
* Selected to direct marketing efforts for manufacturer with $15,000,000 annual sales
* Cited for development of sales campaigns increasing volume 31 %
* Chosen to write sales manual for division of Fortune 500 company
* Appointed to prepare comprehensive advertising programs using variety of media
* Promoted to department manager with $350,000 budget responsibility
* Assigned duties for total staff training including sales
* Elected to national Board of Directors of non-profit health research agency

SKILLS:
= Preparation and monitoring of detailed departmental budgets
= Creative writing ability for all advertising, catalogue, and press release copy
= Devising proposals and bids including GSA and other government agencies
= Composition of photographs and copy to get buyer attention
= Training employees for attainment of maximum performance levels
= Sell products and services using "feature & benefit" approach to meet customer needs
= Identify primary, secondary, and tertiary demographic consumer market areas
= Analyze sales data to determine market penetration and future trends for forecasting revenues
= Profile typical customer by age group, education, income, and gender

ASSETS:

+ Project professional business image situations	+ Dedicated integrity in all
+ Creative problem solving	+ Foster teamwork environment
+ Maintain strict confidentiality	+ Effective communicator
+ Exercise calm, mature judgment	+ Convey confidence
+ Patient in dealing with others	+ Utilize sense of humor
+ Require minimal supervision	+ "Ambassador" to community

Organizational Success Is Job #1

137

John Smith - 1326 S. Alden - Plymouth, MA 00001 - Phone: 700-555-1212

SUMMARY: Professional counseling and teaching experience in business and the humanities with a strong background in post-secondary and adult education.

ACCOMPLISHMENTS:
* Appointed to develop new course proposals that were adopted on submittal
* Assigned as departmental liaison to career planning & placement office
* Chosen to evaluate instructor and program course offerings effectiveness
* Selected to assist dean in review and revision, if needed, of all academic policy
* Elected chair of admissions standards committee
* Cited for designing brochures to attract new students
* Awarded "Outstanding Instructor" of the year
* Evaluated as "highly effective" in all categories by students, peers, and dean

SKILLS:
= Prepare detailed, daily lesson plans prior to the start of each semester
= Write comprehensive course outlines to explain content and expectations for students
= Devise objective and subjective tests for measuring student subject matter retention
= Develop teaching aids such as flip charts and overhead transparencies
= Monitor and evaluate student performance
= Encourage student participation in content discussion
= Advise and counsel students on course selection and major-minor areas
= Meet with students to address their course, college, and personal concerns

SUBJECTS TAUGHT:

Arts & Ideas	Old Testament History (not religion)	Small Business
Art Appreciation	Personnel Management	US History
Supervision	Journalism	English
Salesmanship	The Power of Persuasion	Communications
World History	History of Religions	College Teaching
Marketing	Advertising	Philosophy
Film Making	Script Writing	Tests & Testing

Helping Others To Become Contributing, Participating Members Of Society

138

ELSA F. SCHROEDER

310 East Chart Lane	Algonee, Utah 99974	800 - 555 - 1212

SUMMARY: Dynamic training experience for business, education, and government organizations with an extensive background in the world of work possessing proven problem solving skills for better employee efficiency, performance, and productivity.

ACHIEVEMENTS:
+ Dramatically conduct training sessions being rated "excellent" by 95% of trainees
+ Designed successful training and cross-training programs
+ Developed training video used by hundreds of organizations nation wide
+ Cited for use of multi-media in training presentations
+ Performance of trainees significantly exceeded expectations
+ Devised means to measure training program effectiveness
+ Wrote performance based training manuals
+ Utilized VOJT, JTPA, and TJTC to reduce new employee training costs

TRAINING TOPICS:

Sales	Interviewing	Orientation	Telemarketing
Self assessment	Employee selection	Human resources	Retention
Supervision	Orientation	Motivation	Advertising
Health & safety	Performance evaluation	Team building	Goal setting
Positively positive	Effective communication	Report writing	Budgeting

ABILITIES:
= Analyze employee aptitudes and abilities to determine training needs
= Develop individual and group training plans to improve employee effectiveness
= Prepare appropriate training aids such as slides and overhead transparencies
= Facilitate competency based workshops and seminars using team training approach
= Maintain accurate, detailed records and keep them current
= Test trainees to evaluate progress using pre-test/post-test methods
= Design test instruments, administer, analyze, evaluate, and interpret results

ASSETS:
+ Merit confidence and respect   + Get along well with others
+ Strive for organization success   + Project professional image
+ Keen sense of humor   + Perceptive human evaluations

Proper Training Improves Employee Performance

139

www.ingramcontent.com/pod-product-compliance
Lightning Source LLC
Chambersburg PA
CBHW082229050426
42443CB00033B/3419